SPECTRUM®

Word Problems

Grade 4

Spectrum®
An imprint of Carson Dellosa Education
Greensboro, North Carolina

Spectrum®
An imprint of Carson Dellosa Education
P.O. Box 35665
Greensboro, NC 27425 USA

ISBN 978-1-62442-730-5

04-031227784

Table of Contents Grade 4

Table of Contents, continued

Check What You Know

Adding and Subtracting 1 and 2 Digits

Read the problem carefully and solve. Show your work under each question.

Tanya, Ricardo, Tim, and Sandra participate in their school read-a-thon. They keep track of how many pages they read. After 3 days, Tanya has read 129 pages. Ricardo has read 98 pages. Tim has read 72 pages, and Sandra has read 84 pages.

1. How many pages altogether have Tanya and Ricardo read?

   __227__ pages

   $$\begin{array}{r} 1\ 1 \\ 129 \\ +\ 98 \\ \hline 227 \end{array}$$

   129
   98

2. How many more pages has Tanya read than Tim?

   __57__ pages

   $$\begin{array}{r} 0 \\ \cancel{1}29 \\ -\ 72 \\ \hline 57 \end{array}$$

3. Sandra, Tim, and Ricardo want to know how many pages altogether they have read. How many total pages have they read?

   __254__ pages

   $$\begin{array}{r} 1 \\ 98 \\ +\ 72 \\ 84 \\ \hline 254 \end{array}$$

4. Sandra read more over the weekend. She figures out that she has now read a total of 122 pages for the read-a-thon. How many pages did she read over the weekend? Write the number sentence Sandra can use to check her answer.

   __38__ pages

   $$\begin{array}{r} 0\ 11 \\ \cancel{1}\cancel{2}2 \\ -\ 84 \\ \hline 38 \end{array}$$

   Answer check:

   __122 − 84 could help me find how many pages I read over the weekend and add it to make sure I'm correct__

Lesson 1.1 Adding 1- and 2-Digit Numbers

Read the problem carefully and solve. Show your work under each question.

Jasmine and Aaron collect different types of rocks. Jasmine has 11 rocks in her collection. Aaron has 10 rocks in his collection.

Helpful Hint

To find the sum:

1. add the ones first
2. add the tens next

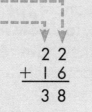

$$\begin{array}{r} 2\ 2 \\ +\ 1\ 6 \\ \hline 3\ 8 \end{array}$$

1. One of Jasmine's sisters gave her 3 rocks. Her other sister gave her 4 more rocks. How many rocks did Jasmine get from her two sisters?

_____7_____ rocks

2. How many rocks does Jasmine have now?

_____18_____ rocks

3. Aaron goes on a school field trip and finds 11 more rocks. How many rocks altogether does he have?

_____21_____ rocks

4. Jasmine and Aaron decide to combine their rock collections. What is the total number of rocks they have?

_____39_____ rocks

$$\begin{array}{r} 2\ 1 \\ +\ 1\ 8 \\ \hline 3\ 9 \end{array}$$

Lesson 1.2 Subtracting 1- and 2-Digit Numbers

Read the problem carefully and solve. Show your work under each question.

Marino is selling raffle tickets. He sold 3 tickets on Monday and 6 tickets on Tuesday. On Wednesday, he sold 16 tickets, and he sold 18 tickets on Thursday.

Helpful Hint

To find the difference:

1. subtract the ones first
2. subtract the tens next

$$\begin{array}{r} 4\ 8 \\ -\ 2\ 6 \\ \hline 2\ 2 \end{array}$$

1. How many more tickets did Marino sell on Tuesday than Monday?

   ___3___ tickets

2. Marino wants to compare the number of tickets he sold on Wednesday to the number of tickets he sold on Tuesday. What is the difference?

   __10 more__ tickets

   6 @ 16

3. How many more tickets did Marino sell on Thursday than Wednesday?

   2
   _____ tickets

4. On Friday, Marino sold 6 fewer tickets than he did on Thursday. How many tickets did he sell on Friday?

   ___12___ tickets

Lesson 1.3 Adding 3 or More Numbers (single digit)

Read the problem carefully and solve. Show your work under each question.

Amit plays a game with his friend Melissa. After four rounds, they decide to stop and add up their points to see who is ahead. Amit's points after four rounds are: 4, 3, 7, and 4. Melissa's points after four rounds are: 8, 3, 3, and 2.

Helpful Hint

When adding 3 or more numbers, look for pairs that are easy to add first:

$$
\begin{array}{r}
6 \\
4 \\
+\ 3 \\
\end{array}
\quad
\begin{array}{r}
1\ 0 \\
+\ 3 \\
\hline
1\ 3 \\
\end{array}
$$

1. How many points does Amit have after four rounds? Which two pairs of numbers should he add first?

   __18__ points

   4+4=8 then 7+3=10

   should be added first.

3. Amit and Melissa play another three rounds. Amit scores 6, 7, and 4 points. How many points does he score during these three rounds?

   __17__ points

   $$
   \begin{array}{r}
   7 \\
   +\ 6 \\
   4 \\
   \end{array}
   \to 10
   $$

   $$
   \begin{array}{r}
   17 \\
   +\ 18 \\
   \hline
   35 \\
   \end{array}
   \to 15
   $$

2. Is Melissa's score higher or lower than Amit's score? How many points does Melissa have?

   Melissa's score is __2 less__ than Amit's score.

   Melissa has __16__ points.

4. Melissa scores 8, 3, and 8 points when she plays three more rounds with Amit. How many points does she score during these three rounds?

   __19__ points

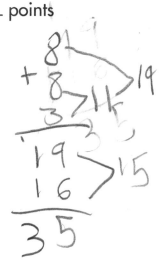

   $$
   \begin{array}{r}
   8 \\
   +\ 8 \\
   3 \\
   \end{array}
   \to 16 \to 19
   $$

   $$
   \begin{array}{r}
   19 \\
   16 \\
   \hline
   35 \\
   \end{array}
   \to 15
   $$

Lesson 1.4 Adding through 2 Digits (with renaming)

Read the problem carefully and solve. Show your work under each question.

Theresa's soccer team had a car wash over the weekend to raise money. On Saturday, the team washed 18 cars before lunch. They washed 26 cars after lunch. On Sunday, the team washed 17 cars before lunch. They washed 19 cars after lunch.

1. How many cars did the team wash on Saturday?

   _44_ cars

   $$\begin{array}{r} 1 \\ 26 \\ +1\ 8 \\ \hline 44 \end{array}$$

2. How many cars did the team wash on Sunday?

   _36_ cars

   $$\begin{array}{r} 1 \\ 19 \\ +17 \\ \hline 36 \end{array}$$

3. How many cars altogether did Theresa's team wash over the weekend?

   _80_ cars

   $$\begin{array}{r} 1 \\ 44 \\ +36 \\ \hline 80 \end{array}$$

Helpful Hint

1. Find the total number of cars the team washed both mornings.
2. Find the total number of cars the team washed both afternoons.
3. Compare both numbers.

4. The team plans to hold another car wash. They want to find out what part of the day they washed the most cars. Did the team wash more cars before or after lunch during both days?

   The team washed more cars

   ___after___ lunch.

Lesson 1.5 Adding Three or More Numbers (2 digit)

Read the problem carefully and solve. Show your work under each question.

Meiko and Carlos want to survey the students at their school. Each grade they plan to survey has three classrooms. Meiko and Carlos listed the number of students in each classroom on the table to the right.

Grade	Number of Students in each Class
Third	20, 18, 19
Fourth	25, 18, 23
Fifth	19, 23, 26
Sixth	21, 25, 23

5^{18} $60\atop9$

1. How many students are in the third grade?

___57___ students

$$\begin{array}{r} 38 \\ + 19 \\ \hline 57 \end{array}$$

2. Which grade has more students, fifth or sixth grade?

The ___Sixth___ grade has more students.

68

6th
> 69

$$\begin{array}{r} 48 \\ + 18 \\ \hline 66 \end{array}$$

3. How many students are in the fourth grade?

___66___ students

$$\begin{array}{r} 137 \\ + 123 \\ \hline 260 \end{array}$$

> **Helpful Hint**
>
> Find the total number of sudents in each grade. Then, add the four amounts together to find the total number of students in all four grades.

4. Meiko and Carlos need to find the total number of students in all four grades. How many students are there?

___260___ students

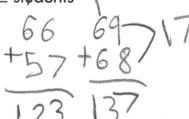

$$\begin{array}{r} 66 \\ + 57 \\ \hline 123 \end{array} \qquad \begin{array}{r} 69 \\ + 68 \\ \hline 137 \end{array}$$

Lesson 1.6 Subtracting 2 Digits from 3 Digits (with renaming)

Read the problem carefully and solve. Show your work under each question.

The Garcia family collected 253 shells on the beach during their summer vacation. Isabella, Marco, and their little sister Maria each want to use some of the shells from the collection for a craft project.

Helpful Hint

To find the difference, subtract the **subtrahend** from the **minuend**. Rename numbers if necessary:

```
                2 15 14
minuend          3  6  4
subtrahend     −    8  7
difference       2  7  7
```

1. Isabella takes 78 shells for her project. How many shells are left in the Garcia family's collection?

_175_ shells

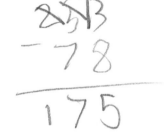

2. After Isabella, Maria takes 47 shells. How many shells are now left in the Garcia family's collection?

_128_ shells

3. Marco plans to use 59 shells for his project. He takes his shells after Isabella and Maria. How many shells are left in the Garcia family's collection?

_69_ shells

4. Isabella's friend Anya also collected shells with her family. Anya's family collected 218 shells. Isabella's family collected 253 shells. What is the difference between the number of shells each family collected?

_35_ shells

Lesson 1.7 Checking Addition and Subtraction Problems

Read the problem carefully and solve. Show your work under each question.

Marisa and her friend Sean each have a baseball card collection. Marisa has 78 cards in her collection. Sean has 113 cards in his collection. Marisa and Sean always keep track of how many cards they have in their collections.

Helpful Hint

Subtraction to check addition:

```
  4 5          7 7
+ 3 2        − 3 2
-----        -----
  7 7          4 5
```

Addition to check subtraction:

```
  1 4 7        1 1 8
−   2 9      +   2 9
-------      -------
  1 1 8        1 4 7
```

1. Marisa gets 23 more baseball cards from her brother. Marisa calculates she now has 101 cards. Write the number sentence Marisa can use to check her answer.

   Subtract 101−23
   or add 78+23

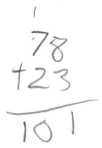

```
  1
  78
+23
----
 101
```

2. Sean gives 18 cards to his friend Alberto. How many cards does Sean have left? Write the number sentence Sean can use to check his answer.

   __95__ cards

   Answer check: subtract 113−18

```
 010
 ✗✗3
 −18
----
  95
```

3. Marisa's cousin Mark has 84 baseball cards. How many more cards does Marisa have than Mark? Write the number sentence Marisa can use to check her answer.

   __17__ cards

   Answer check: do 101−84

```
 0 9
 ✗0✗1
 −84
----
  17
```

Check What You Learned

Adding and Subtracting 1 and 2 Digits

Read the problem carefully and solve. Show your work under each question.

The fourth grade classes collect bottles to recycle. At the end of the week, Mr. Chen's class collected 94 bottles. Ms. Flynn's class collected 132 bottles. Mr. Jackson's class collected 79 bottles, and Ms. Vega's class collected 87 bottles.

---

1. How many bottles altogether did Ms. Flynn's class and Mr. Jackson's class collect?

   __211__ bottles

   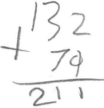
   $$\begin{array}{r} 1\;1 \\ 132 \\ +\;79 \\ \hline 211 \end{array}$$

2. How many more bottles did Ms. Flynn's class collect than Ms. Vega's class?

   __45__ bottles

   $$\begin{array}{r} 0\;12 \\ 1\cancel{3}2 \\ -\;87 \\ \hline 45 \end{array}$$

3. How many bottles altogether did Mr. Chen's, Mr. Jackson's, and Ms. Vega's classes collect?

   __260__ bottles

   $$\begin{array}{r} 2 \\ 94 \\ +87 \\ 79 \\ \hline 260 \end{array}$$

4. The students in Mr. Chen's class brought in more bottles the following week. They had collected a total of 153 bottles to recycle. How many bottles did the students bring in the following week? Write the number sentence Mr. Chen's class can use to check their answer.

   __59__ bottles

   Answer check:

   do 153−94

   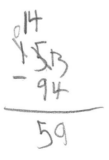
   $$\begin{array}{r} 0\;14 \\ 1\cancel{5}\cancel{3} \\ -\;94 \\ \hline 59 \end{array}$$

CHAPTER 1 POSTTEST

Check What You Know

Numeration through 1,000,000

Read the problem carefully and solve. Show your work under each question.

Toshiro, Leon, Laura, and Inez want to compare the population of the cities where they live. There are 1,068,352 people living in Toshiro's city. Leon's city has a population of 983,832, and Laura's city has a population of 785,342. There are 984,421 people living in Inez's city.

1. What is the value of the number in the hundred thousands place in the population of Laura's city?

_700,000_

3. Leon and Inez decide to compare the populations of both their cities. Compare the two numbers using <, >, or =.

_983,832 < 984,421_

2. Toshiro wants to write the population of his city in expanded form. How is this number written in expanded form?

_1,000,000 + 60,000 +_
_8,000 + 300 + 50 + 2_

How is this number written using number names?

One-million sixty-
eight-thousand
three-hundred fifty-two

4. Toshiro wants to round the population of his city to the nearest ten thousand. What is this number rounded to the nearest ten thousand?

_1,070,000_

all the best
stocking stuffers

A. Truff original hot sauce **17.99**   B. 3pk stacking hot cocoa set **9.99**
C. Neutrogena® 50ct makeup remover cleansing towelettes **10.99**
D. **NEW** Scünci 3-piece Winter Wonderland hair scrunchies **7.99**
E. EOS 2pk vanilla lip balm **4.99**   F. Italian spices **9.99**
Assortment varies by store.

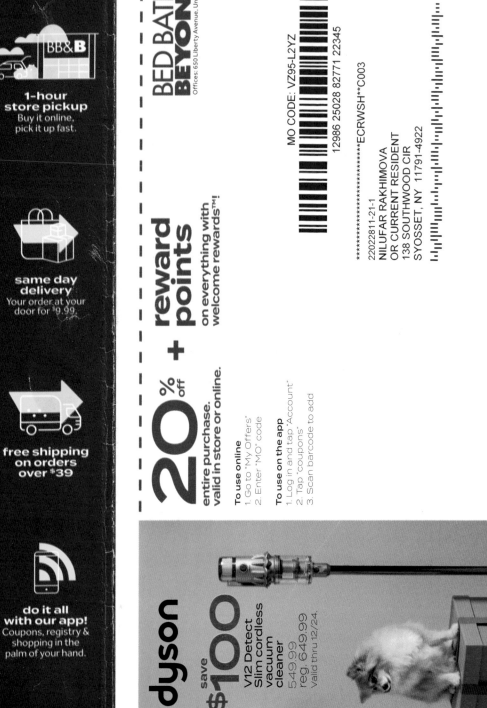

Lesson 2.1 Understanding Place Value (to ten thousands)

Read the problem carefully and solve. Show your work under each question.

Juan researches the science museum and the aquarium in his city. He learns that the science museum had 68,954 visitors last year. The aquarium had 49,703 visitors last year.

Helpful Hint

The value of a digit shows how much it is worth. In the number 532, the digit 5 is in the hundreds place. Its value is 5 hundreds or 500. The value of the 3 is 30.

1. What is the value of the 9 in 68,954?

_____

2. Look at the amount of aquarium visitors. Which digit has a higher value, the 4 or the 7? What is its value?

The _____ has the highest value.

Its value is _____.

3. Juan needs to write the number of science museum visitors in expanded form. What is the expanded form of this number?

_____

_____

How is this number written using number names?

_____

_____

4. What digit is in the thousands place in 49,703? What is its value?

_____ is in the thousands place.

Its value is _____.

Lesson 2.2 Understanding Place Value (to hundred thousands)

Read the problem carefully and solve. Show your work under each question.

Lee and Devin are playing a math game called *Number Spin*. They spin a spinner labeled from 1 to 9. They use each number they spin to make a six-digit number. After the first round, Lee's number is 873,465. Devin's number is 709,456.

1. What is the value of the 7 in Devin's number?

_____

> **Helpful Hint**
>
> The expanded form of a number is written as the sum of the values of each digit in the number.
>
> For example, the expanded form of 4,573 is:
>
> $4,000 + 500 + 70 + 3$

3. How is Lee's number written in expanded form?

_____

_____

2. Whose number has a digit with the highest value in the thousands place, Lee or Devin? What is its value?

_____ has the number with the highest value in the thousands place.

Its value is _____.

4. In the next round, Devin's number was four hundred ninety-one thousand, six hundred twenty-seven. How is this number written in expanded form?

_____

_____

Lesson 2.3 Understanding Place Value (to millions)

Read the problem carefully and solve. Show your work under each question.

Dennis keeps track of facts about his favorite baseball team. He learns that this season 2,670,503 people attended the team's home games. This was a new attendance record. Last season, the attendance was 2,453,091 people.

Helpful Hint

Zeros in a number help to hold a place. They do not have to be included when a number is written in expanded form.

For example, the expanded form of 3,090,001 is:

3,000,000 + 90,000 + 1

1. What is the value of the digit in the millions place in 2,453,091?

_____

2. Which attendance amount has a digit with the highest value in the ten thousands place, this season's or last season's? What is its value?

The attendance amount for

_____ season has the number with the highest value in the ten thousands place.

Its value is _____.

3. Dennis needs to write 2,670,503 in expanded form. How is this number written in expanded form?

_____

_____

4. Dennis predicts that next season's attendance amount will be two million, seven hundred eight thousand, thirty-four. How is this number written in expanded form?

_____

_____

Lesson 2.4 Rounding

Read the problem carefully and solve. Show your work under each question.

Rosa is writing a report about the recent election for the governor of her state. The chart to the right shows how many votes each candidate received.

Candidate	Votes
Mr. Jackson	1,542,690
Ms. Johnson	836,743
Mr. Ramos	123,987

Helpful Hint

To round 3,894 to the nearest thousand:

1. Look at the digit to the right of the thousands place.

2. If this digit is 5 or greater, round up. It is an 8 so the 3 in the thousands place rounds to a 4.

3. Follow with zeros to fill the rest of the places.

1. Rosa wants to round the number of votes Ms. Johnson received. What is this number rounded to the nearest thousand?

_____

2. What is the number of votes Mr. Ramos received rounded to the nearest ten thousand?

_____

3. Rosa rounds the number of votes Mr. Jackson received to the nearest million. What does she get for an answer?

_____

4. What is the number of votes Mr. Ramos received rounded to the nearest hundred?

_____

Lesson 2.5 Greater Than, Less Than, or Equal To

Read the problem carefully and solve. Show your work under each question.

Lee and Devin play *Number Spin* again. This time they change the number of digits in the numbers they create each round. The chart to the right shows the numbers they made for each round.

Round	Lee	Devin
1	34,574	53,046
2	1,942	1,493
3	3,892,356	3,891,936
4	542,002	572,184

Helpful Hint

$<$ means *less than*
$>$ means *greater than*
$=$ means *equal to*

Inequalities are statements in which the numbers are not equal, such as $32 < 42$.

1. Lee and Devin compare their two numbers from round one. Write $<$, $>$, or $=$ to compare their scores.

34,574 _____ 53,046

2. Lee compares the numbers for round two. Show how she compares the two numbers using $<$, $>$, or $=$.

_____

3. Devin writes an inequality statement to compare the numbers in round four. What inequality should he write to compare them?

_____

4. Who won round three, Lee or Devin? Compare their two numbers using an inequality.

_____ won round three.

_____

Check What You Learned

Numeration through 1,000,000

Read the problem carefully and solve. Show your work under each question.

Dennis and his friend David compare some facts about their favorite baseball teams. The home game attendance for Dennis's team this season was 2,670,503 people. David's team had 2,580,490 people attend this season. The average attendance at a home game for Dennis's team is 32,961 people. The average attendance at a home game for David's team is 32,053 people.

1. What is the value of the number in the ten thousands place in 32,053?

_____

2. David needs to write 2,580,490 in expanded form. How is this number written in expanded form?

_____

_____

How is this number written using number names?

_____

_____

3. Dennis and David compare the average attendance at a home game for their two teams. Show how they can compare the two numbers using <, >, or =.

_____

4. Dennis wants to round 2,670,503 to the nearest hundred thousand. What is this number rounded to the nearest hundred thousand?

_____

Check What You Know

Adding and Subtracting 3 through 5 Digits

Read the problem carefully and solve. Show your work under each question.

A local college sells tickets to its football games. The chart to the right shows the number of tickets sold for the first 4 home games.

Game	Number of Tickets Sold
1	945
2	7,495
3	12,587
4	3,899

1. Jamie's family went to the first and third home games. How many tickets altogether were sold for those two games?

_____ tickets

3. Jamie rounds to the nearest thousand to estimate the difference between the number of tickets sold for the third and fourth home game. What is the estimated difference?

about _____ tickets

2. Tom's family went to the second and fourth home games. How many more tickets were sold for the games Jamie's family went to than the games Tom's family went to?

_____ more tickets

4. Tom calculates the total number of tickets sold for the first 4 home games. How many total tickets were sold?

_____ tickets

NAME _____

Read the problem carefully and solve. Show your work under each question.

Dora has a large marble collection. She has 465 purple marbles, 329 blue marbles, 588 green marbles, and 238 clear marbles.

Helpful Hint

When adding 3-digit numbers, first add the ones. Then, add the tens. Finally, add the hundreds.

1. Dora puts all of her blue and green marbles into a jar. How many marbles are in the jar?

_____ marbles

2. Dora puts all of her purple and clear marbles into another jar. How many marbles does she have in this jar?

_____ marbles

3. Dora decides to combine the jar of blue and green marbles with the jar of purple and clear marbles. How many marbles altogether does she have?

_____ marbles

4. Dora gets 125 more blue marbles from her friend. How many blue marbles does Dora have now?

_____ blue marbles

Lesson 3.2 Subtracting through 4 Digits

Read the problem carefully and solve. Show your work under each question.

Olivia, Sonia, and their little brother Max each have been saving pennies. Olivia has 1,978 pennies. Sonia has 2,300 pennies, and Max has 827 pennies.

Helpful Hint

When subtracting a number with zeros in it, remember to rename the places correctly:

Example:

$$
\begin{array}{r}
{\scriptstyle 3\ \ 9\ \ 10} \\
\cancel{4}\ \cancel{0}\ \cancel{0} \\
-\ 1\ 4\ 7 \\
\hline
2\ 5\ 3
\end{array}
$$

1. How many more pennies does Sonia have than Olivia?

_____ pennies

2. Max wants to have the same number of pennies as Olivia. How many more pennies does he need to save?

_____ pennies

3. Olivia gives 402 of her pennies to Max. How many pennies does she have left?

_____ pennies

4. Olivia, Sonia, and Max want to collect a total of 7,500 pennies. They have 5,105 pennies altogether so far. How many more pennies do they need to reach their goal?

_____ pennies

Lesson 3.3 Adding 4- and 5-Digit Numbers

Read the problem carefully and solve. Show your work under each question.

Keiko works at a garden shop. This year, she sold 54,893 packs of flower seeds, 17,463 packs of vegetable seeds, 7,592 outdoor plants, and 3,709 indoor plants.

1. Keiko wants to find out how many total plants she sold. How many outdoor and indoor plants did Keiko sell in all?

_____ plants

Helpful Hint

Use the totals you found from questions one and two to find the total number of items Keiko sold.

3. Keiko needs to find the total number of seed packs and plants she sold this year for her records. How many of these items did she sell in total?

_____ items

2. Keiko decides to reorder more seed packs. How many packs of flower and vegetable seeds altogether did she sell?

_____ seed packs

4. Keiko wants to increase her sale of vegetable seeds for next year. She plans to order double the amount of packs of vegetable seeds she sold. How many packs does she need to order?

_____ packs

Lesson 3.4 Subtracting 4- and 5-Digit Numbers

Read the problem carefully and solve. Show your work under each question.

Roberto and Kim decide to compare the total number of letters and packages the post offices in their hometowns delivered last month. The post office in Roberto's town delivered 54,002 letters and 6,391 packages last month. Kim's town post office delivered 52,083 letters and 7,409 packages last month.

1. Last month, how many more letters did Roberto's town post office deliver than Kim's?

_____ letters

2. What is the difference between the number of packages delivered by the post office in Roberto's town and the number of packages delivered by the post office in Kim's town?

_____ packages

3. Which town post office had the smallest difference between the number of letters and packages it delivered, Roberto's or Kim's?

_____

Helpful Hint

Find and compare the difference between the number of packages each town's post office delivered between last month and this month.

4. This month, Kim's post office delivered 7,803 packages. Roberto's town post office delivered 6,789 packages. Whose town's post office had the greatest increase in package delivery from last month?

_____

Lesson 3.5 Adding 3 or More Numbers (through 4 digits)

Read the problem carefully and solve. Show your work under each question.

Michelle plans a kayaking trip. She researches the lengths of the rivers in her area. She organizes the research in the chart to the right.

River	Length (in miles)
Muddy	745
Rock Island	1,438
Silver	78
Smithville	303

Helpful Hint

When adding numbers with a different number of digits, remember to line the numbers up correctly by place value before adding.

1. Michelle wants to know the total length of the three shortest rivers on the chart. What is the total length of these rivers?

_____ miles

2. What is the total length of the three longest rivers on the chart?

_____ miles

3. Michelle has kayaked on the Silver River, the Rock Island River, and the Muddy River. What is the total length of these three rivers?

_____ miles

Lesson 3.6 Estimating Sums and Differences

Read the problem carefully and solve. Show your work under each question.

A sports team gave away 9,592 free team posters at a recent home game. There were 13,690 fans at the game. At the next home game, the team gave free hats to 8,261 people. There were 13,842 fans at that game.

Helpful Hint

To estimate sums and differences, round each number to the greatest place value the numbers have in common. Then, add or subtract.

$$
\begin{array}{r}
1653 \ \text{-----} \rightarrow \ 1700 \\
+ \ 248 \ \text{-----} \rightarrow \ + \ 200 \\
\hline
1900
\end{array}
$$

1. At the game where free posters were given away, about how many fans did not receive a free poster?

about _____ fans

2. About how many more free posters were given away than free hats?

about _____ more posters

3. The team plans to give away more items at future games. About how many free items were given away at both games in total?

about _____ free items

4. At the game where free hats were given away, about how many fans left the game without a free hat?

about _____ fans

Check What You Learned

Adding and Subtracting 3 through 5 Digits

Read the problem carefully and solve. Show your work under each question.

Yori plans a hiking trip. He researches the heights of the mountains and hills in his area. He organized the heights in the chart to the right.

Name	Height (in feet)
Mt. Cook	8,478
Mt. Herald	3,724
Sky Hill	836
Mt. Cascade	14,784

1. Yori plans to hike Mt. Cascade and Sky Hill in June. What is their total height?

_____ feet

3. Yori wants to estimate the difference in height between Mt. Cascade and Mt. Herald. What is the estimated difference?

about _____ feet

2. Yori plans to hike Mt. Herald and Mt. Cook in July. What is the difference between the combined heights of these mountains and the ones he plans to hike in June?

_____ feet

4. Yori wants to know the combined height of the three mountains and Sky Hill. What is their total height?

_____ feet

Check What You Know

Multiplying through 3 Digits by 2 Digits

Read the problem carefully and solve. Show your work under each question.

Sue's Supply Shop places an order for more office supplies. Sue orders 27 boxes of blue pens. Thirty-five pens come in each box. Paperclips come in boxes of 165, and she orders 37 boxes. She also orders 8 boxes of rulers, and 15 rulers come in each box.

1. Sue plans to have a sale on blue pens. How many blue pens does Sue order in total?

_____ blue pens

3. Sue wants to make sure she has enough space on her shelves for all the rulers she orders. How many rulers altogether does she order?

_____ rulers

2. How many total paperclips does Sue order?

_____ paperclips

4. When Sue receives the order, she finds that 8 of the 27 pen boxes are filled with black pens instead of blue pens. How many blue pens does Sue have from the order?

_____ blue pens

Lesson 4.1 Multiplying Single Digits

Read the problem carefully and solve. Show your work under each question.

Ella makes necklaces for a craft fair. For each necklace, she uses 4 yellow beads, 7 blue beads, 6 red beads, and 8 green beads.

Helpful Hint

To solve a multiplication word problem, you need to find:

1. the number of groups
2. the number of items in each group

1. Ella makes 9 necklaces. How many green beads does she use?

_____ green beads

2. How many yellow beads does Ella use to make the 9 necklaces?

_____ yellow beads

3. To make 6 necklaces, how many red beads does Ella use?

_____ red beads

4. Ella wants to make 8 more necklaces. How many more blue beads will she need? How many more green beads will she need?

_____ blue beads

_____ green beads

Lesson 4.2 Multiplying 2 Digits by 1 Digit

Read the problem carefully and solve. Show your work under each question.

Roger and his friend Aaron like to go mountain biking. They keep track of the total miles they bike each week. Roger bikes 32 miles each week. Aaron bikes 23 miles each week.

Helpful Hint

To find the answer or product:

1. Multiply 3 ones by 2

2. Then, multiply 2 tens by 2

$$
\begin{array}{r}
2\,3 \\
\times\ 2 \\
\hline
4\,6
\end{array}
$$

1. After 3 weeks, how many miles has Roger biked in total?

_____ miles

2. Aaron calculates the total number of miles he biked in 3 weeks. How many miles did he bike?

_____ miles

3. Roger and Aaron bike for another 2 weeks. How many miles did each of them bike during those two weeks?

Roger biked _____ miles.

Aaron biked _____ miles.

4. Roger biked an extra mile each week for 3 weeks. How many total miles did he bike during those 3 weeks?

_____ miles

Lesson 4.3 Multiplying 2 and 3 Digits by 1 Digit (with renaming)

Read the problem carefully and solve. Show your work under each question.

Jerome loves to help take care of the crops on his grandfather's farm. There are 8 rows of tomato plants with 209 plants in each row. The carrots are planted in 9 rows with 47 plants in each row. There are also 7 rows of pepper plants with 106 plants in each row.

Helpful Hint

When multiplying a number with zeros in it, remember to multiply and rename the places correctly:

$$\begin{array}{r} \overset{3}{2}\,0\,8 \\ \times\quad 4 \\ \hline 8\,3\,2 \end{array}$$

1. How many pepper plants are there in all? How many carrot plants are there in all?

_____ pepper plants

_____ carrot plants

2. Jerome loves tomatoes. What is the total number of tomato plants at the farm?

_____ tomato plants

3. Jerome's grandfather wants to add 3 more rows of pepper plants. What is the total number of pepper plants he will add to his crop?

_____ pepper plants

4. Partway through the summer, rabbits ate 2 rows of carrot plants. How many carrot plants are left?

_____ carrot plants

Lesson 4.4 Multiplying 2 Digits by 2 Digits

Read the problem carefully and solve. Show your work under each question.

Ramon's fourth grade class performs a play for their parents. Ramon and other students help set up chairs for the performance. They set up 13 rows of chairs and each row has 21 chairs.

Helpful Hint

To solve two-digit multiplication, first multiply the top number by each of the digits in the bottom number. Then, add the two products together.

$$
\begin{array}{r}
31 \\
\times\ 23 \\
\hline
93 \\
+\ 620 \\
\hline
713
\end{array}
$$

1. How many chairs did the students set up?

_____ chairs

2. The third grade classes are invited to watch. Two rows of chairs are saved for them. How many chairs are left for the parents to use?

_____ chairs

3. Before the play starts, the principal decides to add 2 more chairs to each row. How many total chairs are there now?

_____ chairs

4. The school has another performance next month. There will be 12 rows of 32 chairs. How many total chairs will need to be set up for this performance?

_____ chairs

Lesson 4.5 Multiplying 2 Digits by 2 Digits (with renaming)

Read the problem carefully and solve. Show your work under each question.

Olivia's Orchards grows two types of apples. One type is red and the other is green. The trees that grow red apples are planted in 34 rows with 68 trees in each row. The trees that grow green apples are planted in 26 rows with 47 trees in each row.

Helpful Hint

Remember to add a zero at the end of the second product to show that you are multiplying 31 by 2 tens:

$$
\begin{array}{r}
31 \\
\times\ 23 \\
\hline
93 \\
+\ 620 \\
\hline
713
\end{array}
$$

1. How many of the trees in the orchard grow red apples?

   _____ trees

2. What is the total number of trees in the orchard that grow green apples?

   _____ trees

3. The orchard decides to rope off three rows of red apple trees for a school group to go apple picking. How many red apple trees are not roped off?

   _____ red apple trees

4. Next season, the orchard will add 3 more green apple trees to each row of green apple trees. How many total green apple trees will there be next season?

   _____ green apple trees

Lesson 4.6 Multiplying 3 Digits by 2 Digits (with renaming)

Read the problem carefully and solve. Show your work under each question.

Meiko researches the buildings in her city. The tallest building has 43 floors and 219 windows on each floor. Meiko's father, Mr. Arimoto, works in the building across the street. His building has 27 floors and 128 windows on each floor.

1. How many total windows does the tallest building have?

    _____ windows

3. Window washers washed the windows on 8 floors of Mr. Arimoto's building. How many windows do they have left to wash?

    _____ windows

Helpful Hint

Use the information you know about how many windows are lighted to figure out how many are not lighted per floor.

2. How many total windows does the building Mr. Arimoto works in have?

    _____ windows

4. At night, the tallest building usually keeps the lights on in 107 of its windows on each floor. How many total windows in the building do not keep the lights on?

    _____ windows

Check What You Learned

Multiplying through 3 Digits by 2 Digits

Read the problem carefully and solve. Show your work under each question.

Meiko plans to build models of some of the other buildings in her city. She needs to keep track of the total number of windows per floor and the number of floors for each building. She lists this information in the chart to the right.

Building Name	Number of windows per floor	Number of floors
Ivy Tower	145	28
Jackson Building	95	17
Sky Tower	178	39

1. Meiko plans to make the Jackson Building first. How many windows does it have in all?

_____ windows

3. Which building has the smallest number of windows in all? How many windows does this building have?

The _____
has the smallest number of windows

with _____ windows.

2. Meiko's favorite building is the Ivy Tower. How many windows does it have in all?

_____ windows

4. Meiko learns that the Ivy Tower is fixing the windows on the top 5 floors of the building. How many windows are not being fixed?

_____ windows

Check What You Know

Division Facts through 81 ÷ 9

Read the problem carefully and solve. Show your work under each question.

Darnell collects stickers. He wants to organize them in a sticker book. He plans to put the same number of stickers on each page. Darnell has 24 sports stickers, 81 animal stickers, 36 fuzzy stickers, and 63 scratch-and-sniff stickers.

1. Darnell can fit 9 animal stickers on a page. How many pages will he use for his animal stickers?

_____ pages

3. Darnell fits all of his sports stickers onto 3 pages. If each page has the same number of stickers, how many stickers are on each page? What multiplication sentence can Darnell use to check his division?

_____ stickers

_____

2. Darnell puts all of his scratch-and-sniff stickers on 7 pages. He puts the same number of stickers on each page. How many stickers are on each page?

_____ stickers

4. How many pages will Darnell use for his fuzzy stickers if he puts 6 fuzzy stickers on each page?

_____ pages

Lesson 5.1 Dividing through 45 ÷ 5

Read the problem carefully and solve. Show your work under each question.

Carolyn helps get 4 sailboats ready for a sailing class. She divides the supplies evenly between each sailboat. She has 8 sails and 20 life jackets. All of the sailboats need new ropes for their sails. There are 16 pieces of rope.

Helpful Hint

The division sentence $16 \div 2 = 8$ can also be written as:

quotient − − − − − → 8
divisor − − → $2\overline{)16}$ ← − − dividend

1. Carolyn puts the same number of sails on each boat. How many sails does she put on each sailboat?

   _____ sails

2. The pieces of rope are evenly divided among the boats. How many pieces of rope does each sailboat get?

   _____ pieces of rope

3. Carolyn puts the same number of life jackets on each boat. How many life jackets does she put on each boat?

   _____ life jackets

4. The next sailing class plans to use 8 boats. Carolyn learns that she will need 32 life jackets. How many life jackets will each boat get?

   _____ life jackets

Lesson 5.2 Dividing through 63 ÷ 7

Read the problem carefully and solve. Show your work under each question.

Michael coaches a tennis program at a summer camp. He divides the campers into 2 groups, beginners and advanced. He has 54 tennis balls to use with the beginner group and 48 balls to use with the advanced group. He always divides the tennis balls evenly between each group he puts together.

Helpful Hint

To solve a division word problem, you need to know:
1. the total number of items
2. the number of groups or the number of items in each group

1. Michael divides the beginners into 6 groups for a practice drill. How many tennis balls does each group get?

    _____ tennis balls

2. Michael divides the advanced players into 6 groups to practice serving. How many tennis balls does each group get?

    _____ tennis balls

3. The beginners lost 5 tennis balls. Michael divides the players into 7 groups for the next activity. How many tennis balls will each group get if Michael only has 49 tennis balls?

    _____ tennis balls

4. The advanced players also lost some tennis balls. For their final activity, Michael gives each group 6 tennis balls. How many groups can he make if he only has 42 tennis balls?

    _____ groups

Lesson 5.3 Dividing through $81 \div 9$

Read the problem carefully and solve. Show your work under each question.

Carla fills baskets with flowers for her mom's surprise birthday party. Each of the 8 tables will get a basket. There are 72 pink flowers, 56 yellow flowers, and 64 white flowers. Carla wants to divide the flowers evenly between each basket.

Helpful Hint

To check your answer, use the **inverse**, or opposite, operation. If $81 \div 9 = 9$, then $9 \times 9 = 81$ must be true.

1. Carla evenly divides the pink flowers among the baskets. How many pink flowers are in each basket?

   _____ pink flowers

2. Next, she puts the same number of white flowers in each basket. How many white flowers are in each basket?

   _____ white flowers

3. After Carla evenly divides the yellow flowers among the baskets, she wants to check to make sure she divided correctly. What multiplication sentence can Carla use to check her work?

   _____

4. Carla's sister brought 40 silver ribbons to tie onto the baskets. If the ribbons are divided evenly among all the baskets, how many ribbons will be on each basket?

   _____ ribbons

Check What You Learned

Division Facts through 81 ÷ 9

Read the problem carefully and solve. Show your work under each question.

The marching bands from four area schools are in a large parade. Each band marches in rows with the same number of students in each row. Leo's school band has 45 members. Taro's school band has 72 members. Maya's school band has 32 members, and Barbara's school band has 63 members.

1. Maya's school band marches in 4 rows. How many band members are there in each row?

_____ band members

3. Barbara's band director plans to have 7 rows. How many band members are in each row? What multiplication sentence can be used to check this division?

_____ band members

_____

2. Taro's school band marches with 9 band members in each row. How many rows does the band have?

_____ rows

4. Leo's school band also marches with 9 band members in each row. How many rows does the band have?

_____ rows

Check What You Know

Dividing 2 and 3 Digits by 1 Digit

Read the problem carefully and solve. Show your work under each question.

A bookstore needs to pack books in boxes to ship. Each box can only hold one type of book. Each type of book must be divided evenly between each box. There are 167 nonfiction books and 89 mystery books. There are 35 picture books and 108 fiction books.

---

1. If the mystery books are packed in 6 boxes, how many mystery books will be in each box? How many mystery books will be left over?

_____ mystery books

_____ books left over

2. If 8 picture books can fit into each box, how many boxes can they fill? How many total boxes will the store need to ship all of the picture books? Explain your answer.

_____ full boxes

_____ total number of boxes needed

_____

_____

3. The bookstore plans to use 7 boxes to ship the nonfiction books. How many nonfiction books will fit in each box? How many will be left over?

_____ nonfiction books

_____ books left over

4. The store only has 3 boxes left to ship all the fiction books. Will all the fiction books fit or will there be some left over? Explain your answer.

_____

_____

_____

Lesson 6.1 Dividing 2 Digits

Read the problem carefully and solve. Show your work under each question.

Two different soccer teams need to carpool to the next game. There are 16 players on Molly's team. Each car on Molly's team can hold 5 players. There are 18 players on Lian's team. Each car on Lian's team can hold 4 players. Lian's team has 4 cars.

Helpful Hint

If a number does not divide into another number evenly, there will be a **remainder** (R).

$$\begin{array}{r} 3\,R1 \\ 7\overline{)22} \\ -21 \\ \hline 1 \end{array}$$

1. How many cars can Molly's team fill? How many players will be left over?

_____ full cars

_____ players left

2. How many cars will Molly's team need to take all the players to the game? Explain your answer.

_____ cars

_____

_____

3. Does Lian's team have enough cars to take all their players to the game? If not, how many players still need a ride?

_____

_____

4. Molly's and Lian's coaches combine both teams for a practice drill before the game. They divide all 34 players into groups of three. How many groups of 3 players are there? How many players are left over?

_____ groups of 3

_____ player(s) left

Lesson 6.2 Dividing 3 Digits

Read the problem carefully and solve. Show your work under each question.

Natalia and Manuel have a large stamp collection. They organize their stamps into one album. They put the same number of each type of stamp on a page. Natalia and Manuel have 274 animal stamps, 108 sports stamps, 148 flower stamps, and 324 stamps of famous people and events.

Helpful Hint

Remember to write the first digit of the quotient in the correct spot.

$$7\overline{)434} \quad \frac{62}{}$$

Since $100 \times 7 = 700$ and 700 is greater than 437, there is no hundred digit in the quotient.

1. Natalia wants to use 8 pages of the album for the animal stamps. How many animal stamps will be on each page? How many animal stamps will be left over?

   _____ stamps on a page

   _____ stamps left over

2. Manuel decides to use 4 pages of the album for sports stamps. How many sports stamps will be on each page? How many sports stamps will be left over?

   _____ stamps on a page

   _____ stamps left over

3. Natalia thinks that she can divide all the flower stamps evenly among 5 pages. Will she have enough pages? If not, give the correct amount of pages she will need. Explain your answer.

   _____

   _____

   _____

Check What You Learned

Dividing 2 and 3 Digits by 1 Digit

Read the problem carefully and solve. Show your work under each question.

Kenesha, Shawna, and Jake have postcard collections. They each plan to put their postcards into scrapbooks to organize them. Kenesha has 144 postcards, Shawna has 59 postcards, and Jake has 98 postcards.

1. Shawna only wants to use 9 pages of her scrapbook. How many postcards should she put on each page? How many will be left over?

_____ postcards

_____ postcards left over

2. Jake can fit 4 postcards on each page of his scrapbook. How many pages can he fill with his postcards? If he wants to put all of his postcards in the scrapbook, how many total pages will he need to use?

_____ full pages

_____ total number of pages needed

3. Kenesha plans to put 8 postcards on each page of her scrapbook. How many pages can she fill? How many postcards will be left over?

_____ postcards

_____ postcards left over

4. Kenesha and Shawna decide to combine their postcard collections to make a collage. Each girl will get half of the total number of postcards. How many postcards will each girl get to use in the collage? How many will be left over?

_____ postcards

_____ postcard(s) left over

Mid-Test Chapters 1–6

Read the problem carefully and solve. Show your work under each question.

A construction company plans to remodel a bridge on a busy roadway. The company counts the number of different types of vehicles that use the bridge during one month. After one month, the company counted 32,407 cars, 25,003 small trucks, and 14,598 large trucks. There were also 856 motorcycles and 1,682 vans that used the bridge.

1. How many more small trucks used the bridge than large trucks?

_____ small trucks

3. What is the estimated difference between the number of cars and the number of vans that used the bridge?

about _____

2. What was the total amount of cars, vans, and motorcycles that used the bridge?

_____ cars, vans, and motorcycles

4. How many trucks used the bridge in all?

_____ trucks

Mid-Test Chapters 1–6

Read the problem carefully and solve. Show your work under each question.

Cara works for a publishing company and tracked the sales of two of its best-selling books last year. It sold 9,403,876 copies of a popular picture book and 9,430,523 copies of a popular fiction book.

1. What is the value of the number in the ten thousands place in the number of fiction books sold?

_____

2. Compare the number of picture books and fiction books sold last year using <, >, or =.

_____

3. Cara writes the number of picture books sold in expanded form. How is this number written in expanded form?

_____

_____

4. For her sales report, Cara needs to round the number of picture books to the nearest hundred thousand. What is this number rounded to the nearest hundred thousand?

_____

Mid-Test Chapters 1–6

Read the problem carefully and solve. Show your work under each question.

Aida's Art Shop orders art supplies. Aida orders 29 boxes of small paintbrushes. Twenty-six small paintbrushes come in each box. Drawing pencils come in boxes of 145, and she orders 38 boxes. Aida also orders 9 boxes of colored pencils, and 16 colored pencils come in each box.

1. Aida wants to make sure she has enough room on her shelves for all the small paintbrushes she orders. How many small paintbrushes altogether does she order?

   _____ small paintbrushes

2. Aida plans to have a sale on drawing pencils. How many drawing pencils does she order in all?

   _____ drawing pencils

3. How many total colored pencils does Aida order?

   _____ colored pencils

4. When Aida receives the order, she finds that 7 of the 29 paintbrush boxes are filled with large paintbrushes instead of small ones. How many small paintbrushes did Aida receive from the order?

   _____ small paintbrushes

Mid-Test Chapters 1–6

Read the problem carefully and solve. Show your work under each question.

Pedro works at a paper warehouse. He ships three orders by truck and each order is going to a different place. Pedro wants to put the same number of boxes on each truck. The first order contains 478 boxes of construction paper. The second order contains 833 boxes of drawing paper. The third order contains 83 boxes of poster board.

1. Pedro has 5 trucks available to ship the order of construction paper. How many boxes will he put on each truck? How many boxes will be left?

_____ boxes

_____ boxes left

3. The warehouse has 3 trucks available to ship the order of poster board. How many boxes will Pedro put on each truck? How many boxes will be left?

_____ boxes

_____ boxes left

2. There are 7 trucks ready to ship the order of drawing paper. How many boxes will Pedro put on each truck? How many boxes will be left?

_____ boxes

_____ boxes left

4. Half of the boxes of construction paper in the order have red paper. How many boxes in the order contain red construction paper?

_____ boxes

NAME _____

 Check What You Know

Fractions, Decimals, and Money

Read the problem carefully and solve. Show your work under each question.

Maria and Ramon help paint the youth center in their neighborhood. Maria starts to paint one room blue. Ramon starts to paint one room yellow.

1. Ramon paints $\frac{3}{5}$ of the room before he stops for lunch. Draw a rectangle and shade $\frac{3}{5}$ to show how much of the room he has painted so far.

3. After painting around 3 windows, Ramon has $\frac{2}{3}$ of a can of white paint left. Complete the equivalent fraction below.

$$\frac{2}{3} = \frac{}{9}$$

2. Maria and Ramon take a break and compare how much paint they each have left. Maria has $\frac{5}{8}$ of a can of blue paint left. Ramon has $\frac{7}{8}$ of a can of yellow paint left. Compare the two fractions using $<$, $>$, or $=$.

_____

4. Maria paints $\frac{4}{7}$ of the room blue before she stops for a snack. After her snack, she paints $\frac{2}{7}$ more of the room before she runs out of blue paint. How much of the room has she painted?

_____ of the room

Check What You Know

Fractions, Decimals, and Money

Read the problem carefully and solve. Show your work under each question.

Enrico, Charlie, and Flora collect different sizes of rocks for their science class. They each weigh their rocks in class and compare their results.

1. Charlie's favorite rock weighs $\frac{9}{10}$ of a pound more than Flora's favorite rock. How can $\frac{9}{10}$ be written as a decimal?

_____

3. Charlie and Enrico compare their smallest rocks. Charlie's rock weighs 1.35 pounds. Enrico's rock weighs 0.78 pound. What is the weight difference between these two rocks?

_____ pound

2. Enrico and Flora compare their largest rocks. Enrico's rock weighs 4.29 pounds. Flora's rock weighs 4.92 pounds. Compare the two decimals using <, >, or =.

_____

4. After weighing all the rocks, two of the class scales break. Their teacher, Ms. Leonard, orders two new scales. The large scale costs $24.95, and the small scale costs $17.99. How much do both scales cost in all?

_____

Lesson 7.1 Parts of a Whole

Read the problem carefully and solve. Show your work under each question.

Elizabeth and her brother Jason volunteer to rake yards for some of the people in their neighborhood. Both children rake different neighbors' lawns throughout the week.

Helpful Hint

The **denominator** of a fraction is the total number of equal parts.
The **numerator** of a fraction is the number of parts being counted.

$$\text{numerator} \dashrightarrow \frac{1}{3} \dashleftarrow \text{denominator}$$

1. Elizabeth raked $\frac{1}{2}$ of Mr. Franklin's yard before she had to stop for lunch. Draw a rectangle and shade $\frac{1}{2}$ to show how much of the yard she has raked so far.

2. Jason raked $\frac{1}{3}$ of Ms. Dearman's lawn before it got dark. Draw a rectangle and shade $\frac{1}{3}$ to show how much of the yard he has raked so far.

3. Before soccer practice, Elizabeth raked $\frac{5}{8}$ of Mr. Sanchez's yard. Draw a rectangle and shade $\frac{5}{8}$ to show how much of the yard she has raked so far.

4. One day, Elizabeth and Jason raked their own yard together. They raked $\frac{3}{4}$ of it before lunch. Draw a rectangle and shade $\frac{3}{4}$ to show how much of the yard they have raked so far.

Lesson 7.2 Parts of a Set

Read the problem carefully and solve. Show your work under each question.

John and Kevin went on a 3-day fishing trip with their dad. John caught 5 fish, Kevin caught 4 fish, and their dad caught 9 fish. John kept track of how many trout each of them caught during the trip.

> **Helpful Hint**
>
> Fractions can also be parts of a set or group. The **denominator** is the total number of parts in the set. The **numerator** includes the parts of the set that are shaded.

1. Out of all the fish Kevin caught, $\frac{1}{4}$ of them were trout. Use circles to represent the fish. Draw the total number of fish he caught and shade $\frac{1}{4}$ of the set.

2. Out of all the fish John caught, $\frac{2}{5}$ of them were trout. Use circles to represent the fish. Draw the total number of fish he caught and shade $\frac{2}{5}$ of the set.

3. Out of all the fish John and Kevin's dad caught, $\frac{3}{9}$ of the fish were trout. Use circles to represent the fish. Draw the total number of fish he caught and shade $\frac{3}{9}$ of the set.

4. Last year on the family fishing trip, Kevin caught 3 fish. Two-thirds of the fish Kevin caught were trout. Use circles to represent the fish. Draw the total number of fish he caught last year and shade $\frac{2}{3}$ of the set.

Lesson 7.3 Comparing Fractions

Read the problem carefully and solve. Show your work under each question.

A group of kids are making banners to carry in the town parade. After a few hours, they stop for a break. The kids decide to compare their banners to see how far along they are.

Helpful Hint

If both fractions have the same denominator, look at the numerator to find which fraction is larger.

$$\frac{1}{3} < \frac{2}{3}$$

1. Alberto and Marita compare their banners. Alberto has completed $\frac{3}{5}$ of his banner. Marita has completed $\frac{2}{5}$ of her banner. Compare the two fractions using $<$, $>$, or $=$.

   _____

2. Cheryl has finished $\frac{4}{8}$ of her banner. Bonnie has finished $\frac{6}{8}$ of her banner. Compare the two fractions using $<$, $>$, or $=$.

   _____

3. Melvin and Terry compare their banners. Melvin has finished $\frac{3}{4}$ of his banner so far. Terry has finished $\frac{3}{4}$ of his banner. Compare the two fractions using $<$, $>$, or $=$.

   _____

4. Rob has finished $\frac{2}{7}$ of his banner. Jen has finished $\frac{5}{7}$ of her banner. Compare the two fractions using $<$, $>$, or $=$.

   _____

Lesson 7.4 Mixed Numerals with Like Denominators

Read the problem carefully and solve. Show your work under each question.

People mail various sized letters and packages. The weight of the letters and packages is measured in ounces or pounds. The shipping fees depend on the weight of what is mailed.

Helpful Hint

To add mixed fractions, first add the fractions. Then, add the whole numbers. Finally, reduce the fraction to simplest form.

1. Hector has two packages to mail. One weighs $2\frac{1}{5}$ pounds and the other weighs $3\frac{3}{5}$ pounds. What is the total weight of the packages?

    _____ pounds

2. Natalia has two large letters to send to friends. One weighs $4\frac{3}{8}$ ounces and the other weighs $5\frac{1}{8}$ ounces. How much do the two letters weigh together?

    _____ ounces

3. Tam mailed two packages last week. One weighed $1\frac{4}{5}$ pounds and the other weighed $5\frac{2}{5}$ pounds. How much did they both weigh?

    _____ pounds

4. Jill gets two packages in the mail. One weighs $3\frac{3}{10}$ pounds and the other weighs $6\frac{1}{10}$ pounds. What is the weight of the two packages?

    _____ pounds

5. Hiro sends two letters to friends overseas. One weighs $1\frac{1}{9}$ ounces and the other weighs $4\frac{2}{9}$ ounces. How much do the two letters weigh?

    _____ ounces

Lesson 7.5 Fractions with Like Denominators

Read the problem carefully and solve. Show your work under each question. Write your answer in simplest form.

Jake mows lawns for his summer job. He has mowed $\frac{3}{8}$ of one lawn.

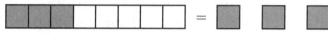

$$= \frac{1}{8} + \frac{1}{8} + \frac{1}{8}$$

---

1. Jake has mowed $\frac{2}{7}$ of another lawn. Draw what this would look like.

3. Jake has mowed $\frac{1}{8}$ of the next lawn. Draw what this lawn would look like.

2. How much of this lawn has Jake mowed?

_____

4. How much of the lawn below does Jake still need to mow?

_____

Lesson 7.6 Finding Equivalent Fractions

Read the problem carefully and solve. Show your work under each question.

Lori and Sam plan to make a collage. They organize the pieces of paper they have by color and shape. Three-fifths of the triangle pieces are blue and $\frac{5}{7}$ of the diamond pieces are yellow. Out of the square pieces, $\frac{16}{24}$ are red. Out of the rectangle pieces, $\frac{12}{15}$ are purple.

Helpful Hint

Equivalent fractions are equal. To find an equivalent fraction, multiply or divide both the numerator and the denominator by the same number.

$$\frac{2}{3} = \frac{2 \times 3}{3 \times 3} = \frac{6}{9}$$

or

$$\frac{10}{12} = \frac{10 \div 2}{12 \div 2} = \frac{5}{6}$$

1. Lori wants to find an equivalent fraction for $\frac{3}{5}$. She multiplies the numerator and the denominator by 4. What equivalent fraction does she get?

_____

2. Sam wants to have 21 diamond pieces. He needs to find how many of these pieces will be yellow if $\frac{5}{7}$ of the diamond pieces are yellow. What is an equivalent fraction for $\frac{5}{7}$?

_____

3. Lori wants to find an equivalent fraction for $\frac{16}{24}$. She divides the numerator and denominator by 8. What equivalent fraction does she get?

_____

4. Sam wants to find an equivalent fraction for the number of purple rectangle pieces. Complete the equivalent fraction below.

$$\frac{12}{15} = \frac{4}{}$$

Lesson 7.7 Adding Fractions with Like Denominators

Read the problem carefully and solve. Show your work under each question.

Dwight starts his homework right after he gets home from school. He wants to get some of it done before soccer practice. His brother Louis also starts his homework right away.

Helpful Hint

Fractions with **like denominators** have the same number in the denominator.

$$\frac{3}{8} + \frac{2}{8} = \frac{3+2}{8} = \frac{5}{8}$$

To add fractions with like denominators, only add the numerators. Write the sum over the common denominator.

---

1. Dwight completes $\frac{2}{8}$ of his math homework before soccer practice. After practice, he completes $\frac{4}{8}$ more. How much of his math homework has he finished?

_____ of his math homework

2. Before his trumpet lesson, Louis finishes $\frac{1}{4}$ of his social studies homework. After his lesson, he finishes $\frac{2}{4}$ more. How much of his social studies homework has he finished?

_____ of his social studies homework

3. Dwight completes $\frac{3}{9}$ of his science project before dinner. After dinner, he finishes $\frac{4}{9}$ more. How much of his science project has he finished?

_____ of his science project

4. Louis writes $\frac{2}{10}$ of his book report before dinner. He writes $\frac{5}{10}$ more after dinner. How much of his book report has he written?

_____ of his book report

Lesson 7.8 Subtracting Fractions with Like Denominators

Read the problem carefully and solve. Show your work under each question.

The wooded area by Emilio's house has 4 walking paths. The Brook Path is $\frac{7}{8}$ of a mile long. The Willow Path is $\frac{8}{9}$ of a mile long. The Bluff Path is $\frac{10}{12}$ of a mile long and the Elm Path is $\frac{5}{6}$ of a mile long. Emilio and his brother Miguel like to walk these paths often.

Helpful Hint

To subtract fractions with like denominators, only subtract the numerators. Write the difference over the common denominator.

$$\frac{8}{10} - \frac{3}{10} = \frac{8-3}{10} = \frac{5}{10}$$

1. Emilio decides to walk down the Willow Path. After walking $\frac{3}{9}$ of a mile, he stops to tie his shoe. How far does he have left to walk?

_____ of a mile

2. Miguel walks $\frac{6}{12}$ of a mile on the Bluff Path before he stops to take a picture. How far does he have left to walk?

_____ of a mile

3. Emilio stops to listen to the babbling brook. He has $\frac{5}{8}$ of a mile left to walk on the Brook Path. How far has he walked?

_____ of a mile

4. Miguel and Emilio both decide to walk down the Elm Path. After walking $\frac{1}{6}$ of a mile, the boys stop to watch an eagle fly by. How far do they have left to walk?

_____ of a mile

Lesson 7.9 Multiplying Fractions and Whole Numbers

Read the problem carefully and solve. Show your work under each question.

The Fully Fit Athletic Club helps its members through aerobic exercises. Each person has a personal plan to work out several times a week. The club keeps records of the amount of time each member spends working out.

Helpful Hint

To multiply a whole number by a fraction, write the whole number as a fraction, such as $7 = \frac{7}{1}$. Then, multiply the numerators. Finally, multiply the denominators.

1. Lisa uses an exercise machine for $\frac{3}{5}$ hour each time she works out. She works out 3 days a week. How many hours does Lisa work out per week?

_____ hours

2. Eddie uses the rowing machine for $\frac{3}{7}$ hour each time he works out. He exercises 5 days a week. How many hours a week does he use the rowing machine?

_____ hours

3. Victor walks rapidly on a treadmill 4 times a week. Each time, he walks for $\frac{4}{9}$ hour. How long does Victor walk on the treadmill each week?

_____ hours

4. Susan swims for $\frac{7}{10}$ hour twice a week. How many hours does Susan swim each week?

_____ hours

5. Anil exercises with a jump rope for $\frac{1}{3}$ hour each visit to the club. He uses the jump rope 6 days a week. How many hours does he exercise with the jump rope each week?

_____ hours

Lesson 7.10 Fraction and Decimal Conversions

Read the problem carefully and solve. Show your work under each question. Write your answer in simplest form.

Mr. Benham's science class grew plants. The students kept track of the height of their plants each day.

Lola's plant grew $\frac{6}{10}$, or 0.6, of a centimeter.

---

1. Lola's plant grew $\frac{6}{10}$ of a centimeter. Tyler's plant grew $\frac{30}{100}$ of a centimeter. How many centimeters did the plants grow altogether?

   _____ centimeters

2. Bailey's plant grew $\frac{3}{10}$ of a centimeter. Eric's plant grew $\frac{40}{100}$ of a centimeter. How many centimeters did the plants grow in all?

   _____ centimeters

   How can this be written as a decimal? _____

3. Sharon's plant grew $\frac{5}{10}$ of a centimeter. How can $\frac{5}{10}$ be written as a decimal?

   _____

4. Lilith's plant grew 0.3 of a centimeter. How can 0.3 be written as a fraction?

   _____

Lesson 7.11 Prime and Composite Numbers

Read the problem carefully and solve. Show your work under each question.

Some students at Terrace Elementary School collect model cars. They make a list of the number of cars each student has. The list is 8, 9, 11, 13, 15, 17, 18, 22, 23, 29, and 31 cars.

Helpful Hint

A number that has only the factors of 1 and itself is a **prime** number. A number with more than two factors is a **composite** number.

A composite number can be written as the product of prime numbers through **prime factorization**:

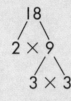

$$18 = 2 \times 3 \times 3$$

1. Jasmine says one number in this group is not a prime number: 11, 13, 15, 17, and 23. Which number is not prime?

_____

2. Morris has 18 model cars. He wants to find a way to arrange them on his shelves. He needs to know all the factors for 18. Write the prime factorization for 18.

_____

3. Flora counts 5 composite numbers in the list. What are the 5 composite numbers?

_____

4. The number of students who collect cars is a prime number. What is the number?

_____

NAME _____

Lesson 7.12 Adding and Subtracting Money

Read the problem carefully and solve. Show your work under each question.

Matt restocks some of the items he sells in his shoe store. He compares the total sales of these items for the past week. The chart to the right shows total sales for the week of some items in his store.

Items	Total Sales
shoes	$1,367.03
sneakers	$874.78
sandals	$325.36
hiking boots	$189.29
socks	$84.18

Helpful Hint

Add and subtract money the same way you add and subtract decimals. Remember to add the decimal point and dollar sign in your answer.

1. Matt compares the weekly sales of sandals and sneakers. What is the difference?

   _____

2. Matt wants to find the combined total of the shoes and sneakers sold for the week. What is the total?

   _____

3. What is the difference in weekly sales between the hiking boots and the sandals?

   _____

4. What is the weekly sales total for sneakers and socks?

   _____

Check What You Learned

Fractions, Decimals, and Money

Read the problem carefully and solve. Show your work under each question.

Tamika and Franklin are both reading the same book. They each keep track of how much of the book they have read so far. They also compare how much they each have read.

1. Tamika read $\frac{1}{4}$ of her book during the first two days she started reading. Draw a rectangle and shade $\frac{1}{4}$ to show how much of the book she has read so far.

3. One day, Tamika spent $\frac{3}{4}$ of an hour reading her book. Complete the equivalent fraction below.

   $$\frac{3}{4} = \frac{}{20}$$

2. After the first week, Tamika and Franklin compare how much of the book they have each read so far. Tamika has read $\frac{4}{6}$ of the book. Franklin has read $\frac{3}{6}$ of the book. Compare the two fractions using $<$, $>$, or $=$.

   _____

4. Franklin has $\frac{3}{6}$ of his book left to read. He reads $\frac{1}{6}$ of that amount over the weekend. How much of the book does he have left to read?

   _____ of his book left

Check What You Learned

Fractions, Decimals, and Money

Read the problem carefully and solve. Show your work under each question.

Stacy and Chelsea plan to make beaded bracelets and necklaces for their friends and families. Both girls collect all the materials before they start.

1. A medium-sized bag of beads weighs $\frac{8}{10}$ of a pound more than the small-sized bag. How can $\frac{8}{10}$ be written as a decimal?

_____

2. Stacy and Chelsea each decide to make a bracelet first. They each cut a length of black cord on which to string the beads. Stacy's cord is 21.86 centimeters long. Chelsea's cord is 21.68 centimeters long. Compare the two lengths using $<$, $>$, or $=$.

_____

3. Chelsea makes a necklace. She cuts a black cord that measures 45.14 centimeters long. She compares it to the length of the cord Stacy cut for a bracelet, which was 21.86 centimeters long. What is the difference in length between the cords for the bracelet and the necklace?

_____ centimeters

4. The girls spent $12.99 on bags of different colored beads. They also spent $4.56 on the roll of black cord. What was the total amount of money they spent?

_____

CHAPTER 7 POSTTEST

Check What You Know

Customary Measurement

Read the problem carefully and solve. Show your work under each question.

The Davis family wants to plant a garden in their backyard. Dylan and his younger brother Otis help their parents prepare the garden before planting.

1. Dylan and his mom dig a rectangular section of dirt for the garden. They also plan to put a fence around it to keep the dog out. The garden is 6 feet long and 4 feet wide. What is the area of the garden? What is the perimeter?

   The area of the garden is

   _____ square feet.

   The perimeter of the garden is

   _____ feet.

2. Dylan finds that there are 12 feet of fencing left over from the garden. His dad wants to use it in other parts of the yard. How many yards of fencing are left over?

   _____ yd.

3. Dylan's dad pours a 5-pound bag of fertilizer onto the garden. How much does the bag weigh in ounces?

   _____ oz.

4. Otis waters the garden after all the plants are in the ground. The watering can he uses holds 5 quarts of water. How many pints of water does it hold?

   _____ pt.

Lesson 8.1 Measuring Inches

Read the problem carefully and solve. Show your work under each question.

Tamora needs to make a poster for a school project. She uses a pencil so that she can erase any mistakes. Tamora also uses a ruler to help her draw some straight lines.

Helpful Hint

The lines on the ruler help you measure to the nearest $\frac{1}{2}$ inch, $\frac{1}{4}$ inch, and $\frac{1}{8}$ inch.

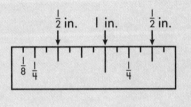

1. What is the length to the nearest $\frac{1}{2}$ inch of Tamora's pencil below?

_____ in.

2. Tamora draws a straight line that is $1\frac{1}{4}$ inches long. Use a ruler to draw this line below.

3. Tamora drew the rectangle below. What is its length to the nearest $\frac{1}{8}$ inch?

_____ in.

4. Tamora draws another straight line that is $2\frac{1}{8}$ inches long. Use a ruler to draw this line below.

Lesson 8.2 Units of Length (inches, feet, yards, and miles)

Read the problem carefully and solve. Show your work under each question.

Rosa and Nancy plan to make a quilt. They need to buy fabric at the store. They buy blue, green, and yellow fabric.

Helpful Hint

1 foot (ft.) = 12 inches (in.)

1 yard (yd.) = 3 feet (ft.) = 36 inches (in.)

1 mile (mi.) = 1,760 yards (yd.) = 5,280 feet (ft.)

When converting from a larger unit to a smaller unit, multiply. When converting from a smaller unit to a larger unit, divide.

1. Rosa and Nancy need 108 inches of green fabric. How many yards of green fabric do they need?

   _____ yd.

2. Nancy buys 7 yards of blue fabric. How many feet of blue fabric does she buy?

   _____ ft.

3. Rosa buys 4 feet of yellow fabric. How many inches of yellow fabric does she buy?

   _____ in.

4. The fabric store is 3 miles away from Nancy's house. How far away is the store in feet?

   _____ ft.

Lesson 8.3 Units of Length (feet and inches)

Read the problem carefully and solve. Show your work under each question.

Mrs. Wilson's class is recording how tall they are for a math project. Complete the chart below and then answer the questions.

I.

Feet	Inches
1	12
2	24
3	
4	
5	
6	

3. Mindy is 61 inches tall. How tall is she in feet and inches?

_____ ft. _____ in.

2. Jake is 4 feet 8 inches tall. How tall is he in inches?

_____ in.

4. Tomas is 4 feet 6 inches tall. How tall is he in inches?

_____ in.

Lesson 8.4 Measurements in Fractions of a Unit

Read the problem carefully and solve. Show your work under each question.

A group of students measured their index fingers to the nearest $\frac{1}{4}$ inch. Display the data on the line plot below.

1.

1. Justin 4	4. Sandy $3\frac{1}{4}$
2. Rob $3\frac{1}{4}$	5. Brittany $2\frac{1}{2}$
3. John $3\frac{1}{4}$	6. Amanda $2\frac{1}{4}$

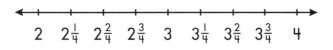

2. What is the difference between the longest and shortest finger?

_____ in.

3. What is the most common finger size?

_____ in.

4. How many measurements are less than $3\frac{1}{2}$ inches?

_____

Lesson 8.5 Liquid Volume (cups, pints, quarts, and gallons)

Read the problem carefully and solve. Show your work under each question.

Bernardo sells homemade lemonade at the town fair. He sells containers in quart and gallon sizes. He also sells individual cups of lemonade.

Helpful Hint

Use the following information to convert units of liquid volume:

1 cup (c.) = 8 ounces (oz.)
1 gallon (gal.) = 4 quarts (qt.)
1 pint (pt.) = 2 cups (c.)
1 gallon (gal.) = 8 pints (pt.)
1 quart (qt.) = 2 pints (pt.)
1 gallon (gal.) = 16 cups (c.)
1 quart (qt.) = 4 cups (c.)

1. Mr. Wong wants 6 pints of lemonade. How many quarts does he need to buy?

_____ qt.

2. Bernardo uses a pitcher to pour the individual cups of lemonade. The pitcher can fill 4 cups before it needs to be refilled. How many ounces can it fill?

_____ oz.

3. Mrs. Foster needs 12 quarts of lemonade. Bernardo suggests she buy the gallon containers instead. How many gallons does she need to buy?

_____ gal.

4. Mr. Santos buys 3 gallons of lemonade to serve at a party. How many cups can he serve with 3 gallons of lemonade?

_____ c.

Lesson 8.6 Weight (ounces, pounds, and tons)

Read the problem carefully and solve. Show your work under each question.

Christina often visits the local zoo with her family. She likes to learn interesting facts about her two favorite animals at the zoo, the African elephant and the tiger.

Helpful Hint

Use the following information to convert units of weight:

1 pound (lb.) = 16 ounces (oz.)
1 ton (T.) = 2,000 pounds (lb.)

1. Christina learns that the male African elephant at the zoo weighs 6 tons. How many pounds equal 6 tons?

_____ lbs.

2. Christina also finds out that the female African elephant at the zoo weighs 6,000 pounds. How many tons does it weigh?

_____ T.

3. Christina learns that one of the new baby tigers at the zoo weighed 2 pounds when it was born. How many ounces did it weigh?

_____ oz.

4. Christina also learns that one of the female tigers at the zoo weighs 300 pounds. What is this weight in ounces?

_____ oz.

Lesson 8.7 Measuring Perimeter

Read the problem carefully and solve. Show your work under each question.

Russell's rug company makes and sells many types of rugs. Some of the rugs have fringe around all four sides. The rugs with fringe come in 3 different sizes. Russell needs to order more fringe. First, he has to find the perimeter of each rug to know how much fringe each rug needs.

Helpful Hint

Perimeter is the distance around a shape. To find the perimeter, add together the lengths of all the sides.

1. Russell finds the perimeter of the small rug. This rug is 6 feet long and 4 feet wide. How much fringe will he need for this rug?

   _____ ft.

2. The medium-sized rug is 8 feet long and 6 feet wide. What is the perimeter of this rug?

   _____ ft.

3. Russell finds the perimeter of the large rug. This rug is 12 feet long and 10 feet wide. How much fringe will he need for this rug?

   _____ ft.

4. Russell learns that his company wants to put fringe around one size of their square rugs. This rug has sides that measure 4 feet long. How much fringe will he need for this rug?

   _____ ft.

Lesson 8.8 Measuring Area

Read the problem carefully and solve. Show your work under each question.

Russell's rug company also sells carpets that are cut to fit the size of a room. Customers give the measurements of the room. Russell then finds the area of the room so he knows how many square feet of carpeting he will need.

Helpful Hint

To find the **area** of a square or rectangle, multiply its length by its width.

30 ft. × 20 ft. = 600 sq. ft.

The product is written in square feet.

1. One customer needs carpet for a rectangular room that is 7 feet long and 6 feet wide. Russell finds the area of the room. How much carpeting does he need?

_____ sq. ft.

2. Russell receives an order for a rectangular carpet that needs to be 14 feet long and 8 feet wide. What is the area of the carpet?

_____ sq. ft.

3. Another customer has a square room that she wants to carpet. The length of one of the sides is 6 feet. How much carpeting will she need?

_____ sq. ft.

4. Russell receives an order for 72 square feet of carpeting for a rectangular room. His paperwork says that the room is 9 feet long. However, the measurement for width of the room is smudged. What is the width of the room?

_____ ft.

Check What You Learned

Customary Measurement

Read the problem carefully and solve. Show your work under each question.

Christina and her family make another trip back to the local zoo. This time, Christina's younger sister Jenny comes with them. Jenny's favorite animal is the hippopotamus. She wants to go to the hippo area right away.

1. The girls learn that the zoo added a second pool for the hippos. The new rectangular pool is 24 feet long and 9 feet wide. What is the area of this pool? What is its perimeter?

   The area of the pool is _____ square feet.

   The perimeter of the pool is

   _____ feet.

3. Jenny and Christina's mom brought a thermos of water for them to drink. The thermos holds 3 quarts of water. How many cups does it hold?

   _____ c.

4. Christina wants to go see the tigers next. The tiger pen is 15 yards away from the hippo area. What is this distance in feet?

   _____ ft.

2. Jenny learns that the male hippo at the zoo weighs 3 tons. How many pounds does it weigh?

   _____ lb.

NAME _____

 Check What You Know

Metric Measurement

Read the problem carefully and solve. Show your work under each question.

Mr. Chang is remodeling his backyard. He is adding a swimming pool and deck for his family to enjoy. He also plants flowers along the side of the deck.

1. Mr. Chang builds a rectangular swimming pool. The pool is 9 meters long and 4 meters wide. What is the perimeter of the pool? What is the area of the pool?

The perimeter of the pool is

_____ meters.

The area of the pool is _____ square meters.

3. After the pool and deck are built, Mr. Chang makes a path between them. He uses crushed stones to make the path. One bag of crushed stones weighs 7 kilograms. What does the bag of crushed stones weigh in grams?

_____ g

2. Mr. Chang reads the plans for the deck. The deck will be 3 meters long. What is the length of the deck in centimeters?

_____ cm

4. Mr. Chang waters the flowers along the side of the deck. His watering can holds 3 liters of water. How many milliliters does the watering can hold?

_____ mL

NAME

Lesson 9.1 Measuring in Centimeters and Millimeters

Read the problem carefully and solve. Show your work under each question.

Juanita draws a model of her room using shapes and lines. She measures and labels all the lines in centimeters or millimeters.

Helpful Hint

Use the following information to convert lengths to centimeters or millimeters:

1 centimeter (cm) = 10 millimeters (mm)

1. Juanita draws a straight line that is 4 centimeters long. Use a ruler to draw this line below.

3. Juanita drew part of her rectangular desk below. Use a ruler and a pencil to finish her drawing. Find the length of the missing side in millimeters.

_____ mm

2. Juanita draws a line that is 12 centimeters to model the length of one side of her room. What is the length of the line in millimeters?

_____ mm

4. Juanita draws another line that is 90 millimeters long. What is the length of the line in centimeters?

_____ cm

Lesson 9.2 Meters and Kilometers

Read the problem carefully and solve. Show your work under each question.

Derek has several chores to do before soccer practice. He has to clean the kitchen, vacuum the living room, and walk the dog.

Helpful Hint

Use the following information to convert lengths to meters or kilometers:

100 centimeters (cm) = 1 meter (m)
1,000 meters (m) = 1 kilometer (km)

1. Derek cleans the kitchen counter. The counter is 300 centimeters long. How long is the counter in meters?

_____ m

2. Derek vacuums the living room rug. The rug is 4 meters long. How long is the rug in centimeters?

_____ cm

3. Derek takes his dog for a walk. They walk 2,000 meters. How many kilometers did they walk?

_____ km

4. Derek's mom drives him to soccer practice. The soccer field is 8 kilometers away. How far away is the soccer field in meters?

_____ m

Lesson 9.3 Units of Length (millimeters, centimeters, meters, and kilometers)

Read the problem carefully and solve. Show your work under each question.

Derek's sister Cora has chores to do before her piano lesson. She needs to clean her room and finish her math homework.

Helpful Hint

1 centimeter (cm) = 10 millimeters (mm)
1 meter (m) = 1,000 millimeters (mm)
1 meter (m) = 100 centimeters (cm)
1 kilometer (km) = 1,000 meters (m)

1. Cora sharpens her pencil before she starts her math homework. Her pencil is now 15 centimeters long. How long is the pencil in millimeters?

_____ mm

2. Cora sweeps the floor in her room. One side of her room is 300 centimeters long. How many meters long is her room?

_____ m

3. Cora cleans one shelf in her closet. The shelf is 2 meters long. What is its length in millimeters?

_____ mm

4. Cora's dad drives her from their house to her piano lesson at the community center. The community center is 4 kilometers from their house. How many meters is the community center from their house?

_____ m

Lesson 9.4 Liquid Volume (milliliters)

Read the problem carefully and solve. Show your work under each question.

Oliver's Orchards sells apple cider in different-sized bottles. The amount of cider in each bottle is measured in liters.

Helpful Hint

Liquid can be measured in liters and milliliters:

1 liter (L) = 1,000 milliliters (mL)

1. One customer bought a 2-liter bottle of cider. How many milliliters of cider does the bottle hold?

   _____ mL

2. Oliver has a sale on 4-liter bottles of cider. How many milliliters does this size bottle hold?

   _____ mL

3. The Smith family bought a few bottles of cider. The total amount of liters of cider they bought is 14 liters. How many milliliters is this?

   _____ mL

4. Andrew is planning a party. He needs 18,000 milliliters of cider. How many liters of cider does he need?

   _____ L

Lesson 9.5 Weight (milligrams, grams, and kilograms)

Read the problem carefully and solve. Show your work under each question.

Mario plans a camping trip. Once he gets to the parking lot, he will need to carry all of his supplies to his campsite. Before he leaves, Mario decides to weigh some of his supplies so he will know how much he will have to carry.

Helpful Hint

Weight can be measured in milligrams, grams, and kilograms:

1 gram (g) = 1,000 milligrams (mg)
1 kilogram (kg) = 1,000 grams (g)

1. Mario's backpack weighs 2,000 grams. How many kilograms does it weigh?

   _____ kg

2. Mario made 300 grams of trail mix to take on the camping trip. What is the weight of the trail mix in milligrams?

   _____ mg

3. Mario's tent weighs 5 kilograms. How many grams does it weigh?

   _____ g

4. Mario's favorite animal is a deer. A male deer weighs around 135 kilograms. What is this weight in grams?

   _____ g

Lesson 9.6 Time

Read the problem carefully and solve. Show your work under each question.

Tim wrote a schedule of his workouts for last week. He ran, biked, swam, and hiked.

> **Helpful Hint**
> There are 60 minutes in an hour.

1. On Monday, Tim ran for 1 hour and 15 minutes. How many minutes did he run?

   _____ minutes

2. Tim biked for 2 hours and 12 minutes on Tuesday. How many minutes did he bike?

   _____ minutes

3. On Friday, Tim swam for 1 hour and 35 minutes. How many minutes did he swim?

   _____ minutes

4. Tim hiked for 3 hours and 20 minutes on Saturday. How many minutes did he hike?

   _____ minutes

Check What You Learned

Metric Measurement

Read the problem carefully and solve. Show your work under each question.

Caroline visits the aquarium with her family. Every time she goes to the aquarium, she likes to visit the new exhibits. She also likes to look at the different animals and learn interesting facts about them.

1. Caroline's favorite animal is the dolphin. One of the dolphins in the tank is 4 meters long. What is its length in centimeters?

_____ cm

3. Caroline reads fun facts about sea creatures. She learns that a giant squid can weigh 200 kilograms. What is this weight in grams?

_____ g

2. Caroline learns that another rectangular pool was built for the penguin exhibit. The pool is 12 meters long and 7 meters wide. What is the perimeter of the pool? What is its area?

The perimeter of the pool is

_____ meters.

The area of the pool is _____ square meters.

4. On the way home from the aquarium, Caroline's mother buys a 5-liter bottle of water. How many milliliters of water does the bottle hold?

_____ mL

NAME _____

Check What You Know

Graphs and Probability

Read the problem carefully and solve. Show your work under each question.

Mr. Perez's class collects cans of food for a food drive. After the first four days, the class makes a graph to show how many cans of food they collected each day.

1. On which day of the week did the students collect the most cans of food?

   _____

2. How many cans of food did the students collect on Wednesday?

   _____ cans of food

3. How many more cans of food did the students collect on Monday than on Thursday?

   _____ more cans of food

4. Carmen and Harry pack 12 cans of food into a box. Five of the cans contain vegetables. Seven of the cans contain soup. If Harry pulls one of the cans out of the box without looking, what is the probability that it will be a soup can?

   _____

Check What You Know

Graphs and Probability

Read the problem carefully and solve. Show your work under each question.

Cathy and Benito sell calendars to raise money for a local charity. They sell two types of calendars: desk calendars and pocket calendars. After four weeks, they decide to make a graph that shows the total calendar sales each week.

Calendar Sales

1. During which week did Cathy and Benito sell the most calendars?

   week _____

2. How many calendars did they sell during the second week?

   _____ calendars

3. During which two weeks did they sell the same number of calendars?

   weeks _____ and _____

4. Cathy and Benito pack the 25 calendars they have not sold into a box. There are 16 desk calendars and 9 pocket calendars in the box. If Benito pulls a calendar out of the box without looking, what is the probability that it will be a pocket calendar?

   _____

Lesson 10.1 Reading Bar Graphs

Read the problem carefully and solve. Show your work under each question.

Carlos and Michaela decide to survey the fourth-grade students. They ask the students what season they like best. Carlos and Michaela make a graph of their results. The bar graph to the right shows the data from the survey.

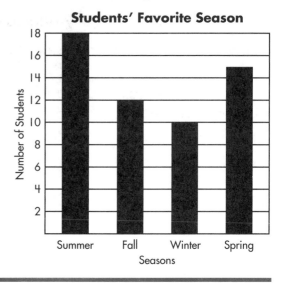

Students' Favorite Season

Helpful Hint

A **bar graph** is used to compare data. The data is shown on the graph using rectangular bars.

1. Which season was chosen the most favorite by the students in the fourth grade?

   _____

2. How many students chose spring as their favorite season?

   _____ students

3. Which season was chosen as the least favorite according to the graph?

   _____

4. How many more students chose summer as their favorite season than fall?

   _____ more students

Lesson 10.2 Reading Line Graphs

Read the problem carefully and solve. Show your work under each question.

Jamie trains for her first race. She tracks how many miles she runs each week. After four weeks, she makes the line graph to the right to show her progress.

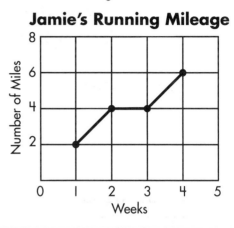

Jamie's Running Mileage

Helpful Hint

A **line graph** is used to show changes in data over time. The information is shown using points on the graph. A line connects all the points.

1. During which week did Jamie run the greatest number of miles?

week _____

2. How many miles did Jamie run during the first week of her training?

_____ miles

3. During which two weeks did Jamie run the same number of miles?

weeks _____ and _____

4. How many more miles did Jamie run during the fourth week than during the first week of her training?

_____ more miles

Lesson 10.3 Probability

Read the problem carefully and solve. Show your work under each question.

Jamal and his sister Keisha play a board game. They use the spinner to the right to see how many spaces to move on each turn. They calculate the probability of spinning certain numbers as they play.

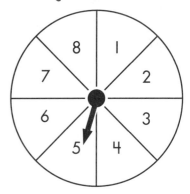

Helpful Hint

Probability is the chance of an event occurring.

The probability of an event can be described using a fraction:

$$\text{Probability} = \frac{\text{number of favorable outcomes}}{\text{total number of possible outcomes}}$$

1. Jamal will be ahead of Keisha if he can spin a 7. What is the probability that he will spin a 7?

_____

2. Keisha hopes to spin a number that is 5 or less. What is the probability that she will spin a number less than or equal to 5?

_____

3. Jamal wants to spin an even number. What is the probability of the spinner landing on an even number?

_____

4. Keisha can win if she spins a 3 or a 4. What is the probability that she will spin a 3 or a 4?

_____

NAME _____

Check What You Learned

Graphs and Probability

Read the problem carefully and solve. Show your work under each question.

Mr. Franklin's class enjoys going to the school library each week. The librarian, Mrs. Ryan, made the graph to the right to show the number of books the students in Mr. Franklin's class checked out during one week.

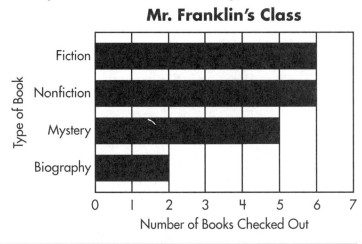

Mr. Franklin's Class

1. The students checked out the greatest number of books from two types of books in the library. Which two types of books were checked out the most?

   _____ and

   _____

2. How many mystery books did the students check out?

   _____ mystery books

3. How many more nonfiction books were checked out than biography books?

   _____ more nonfiction books

4. Mrs. Ryan receives an order of 20 new books for the library. Thirteen of the books in the box are fiction and 7 are nonfiction. If Mrs. Ryan selects a book from the box without looking, what is the probability that she will select a fiction book?

   _____

Check What You Learned

Graphs and Probability

Read the problem carefully and solve. Show your work under each question.

Jeremy and the other fourth grade students at his school sell raffle tickets. Jeremy's teacher asks him to make a graph showing the total number of raffle tickets sold each week.

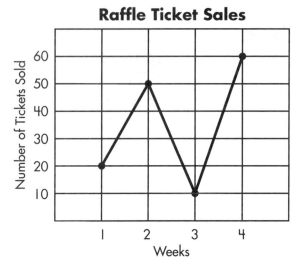

Raffle Ticket Sales

1. During which week did the students sell the smallest number of raffle tickets?

   week _____

2. How many raffle tickets did the students sell during the fourth week?

   _____ tickets

3. How many more tickets did the students sell during the second week than during the third week?

   _____ more tickets

4. The fourth grade sold a total of 140 raffle tickets. Jeremy's family bought 11 raffle tickets. What is the probability that Jeremy's family will win the raffle?

   _____

Check What You Know

Geometry

Read the problem carefully and solve. Show your work under each question.

Jared draws a model of the inside of his school using a grid. He uses a ruler to draw straight lines and angles.

1. Jared plots a point on the grid below. What ordered pair represents this point?

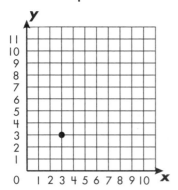

_____

3. Jared uses parallel lines to show a hallway in the school. Draw a pair of parallel lines in the space below.

2. Jared decides to draw a ray using the point he just made. Use the point in the grid above to draw a ray.

4. Jared draws the angle below. Identify this angle as a right angle, an obtuse angle, or an acute angle.

_____

NAME _____

Check What You Know

Geometry

Read the problem carefully and solve. Show your work under each question.

Carlota draws a design in art class. She uses several different polygons in her design. When she is finished drawing her design in pencil, she plans to paint it.

1. Carlota draws the polygon below. What is the name of this polygon?

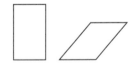

_____

2. Carlota draws the two polygons below. Identify the shapes as congruent or not congruent.

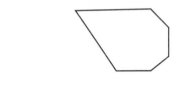

_____

3. Carlota draws the two triangles below. She draws the triangle on the left first. Is the triangle on the right a slide, flip, or turn of the triangle on the left?

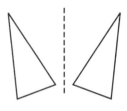

_____

4. When Carlota finishes her design, she gets a can of blue paint. The can of paint reminds her of the solid figure below. What is the name of this figure?

_____

NAME _____

Lesson 11.1 Plane Figures

Read the problem carefully and solve. Show your work under each question.

The students in Ms. Gomez's class study various polygons. She has them play a geometry guessing game in pairs. One of the partners is secretly given a polygon. This student has to give clues to make his or her partner guess the correct polygon.

Helpful Hint

Polygons are closed-plane figures with 3 or more straight sides. Some examples of polygons are:

triangle	3 sides
quadrilateral	4 sides
pentagon	5 sides
hexagon	6 sides
heptagon	7 sides
octagon	8 sides
nonagon	9 sides

1. Camila says her polygon has 8 sides. What is the name of her polygon?

_____

2. Taro says his polygon has 5 sides. Name and draw his polygon below.

_____

3. Peter says his polygon has 6 sides. Name and draw his polygon below.

_____

4. Mina drew her polygon below. What is the name of her polygon?

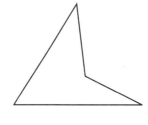

_____

Lesson 11.2 Solid Figures

Read the problem carefully and solve. Show your work under each question.

The students in Ms. Gomez's class play another round of the geometry guessing game. This time, the students have to guess the correct solid figure. One partner shows a picture of the solid figure and the other partner has to guess its correct name.

Helpful Hint

Solid figures have 3 dimensions. They can appear hollow or solid. Some examples of solid figures are:

cylinder   rectangular prism
cone   square pyramid
cube   sphere

1. Jose shows the solid figure below to his partner. What is the name of his figure?

_____

2. Gina shows the solid figure below to her partner. What is the name of her figure?

_____

3. Alan's solid figure is shown below. He shows it to his partner to help him guess. What is the name of the figure?

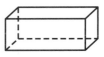

_____

4. Patty shows the solid figure shown below to her partner. What is the name of her figure below?

_____

Lesson 11.3 Congruent Figures

Read the problem carefully and solve. Show your work under each question.

Julieta and Mori make a poster. They want to design a border on it using congruent shapes. They each decide to draw different figures to see which ones they like best for the poster.

> **Helpful Hint**
>
> Two shapes are **congruent** if they are exactly the same size and shape.

1. Julieta draws the two shapes below. Identify the shapes as congruent or not congruent.

_____

2. Mori draws the two circles below. Are they congruent or not congruent?

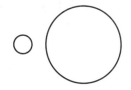

_____

3. Julieta likes the two shapes below for a border. Are the two shapes congruent or not congruent?

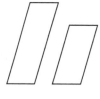

_____

4. Mori wants to use the two rectangles below for a border. Are these shapes congruent or not congruent?

_____

Lesson 11.4 Slides, Flips, and Turns

Read the problem carefully and solve. Show your work under each question.

Anita, Paul, and Hana draw pattern designs using a shape stencil. They each draw one shape, then move the stencil to draw the same shape in a different position. Paul uses a triangle for his design and Hana uses a rectangle. Anita starts her design by drawing the pattern to the right. She draws the top shape first.

Helpful Hint

A **slide** moves a figure up, down, left, right, or diagonally.

A **flip** creates a mirror image.

A **turn** rotates a figure around a point.

1. Did Anita slide, flip, or turn the second shape to make her design?

_____

2. Paul decides to flip his second triangle to make his design. Draw a second triangle on the right side to show how he flips it.

3. Hana decides to slide her second rectangle to the right to make her design. Draw a second rectangle to show how she slides it up and to the right.

4. Hana makes a second design using the same shape. This time, she decides to turn it. Draw a rectangle using the dot to show how Hana could turn her shape.

Lesson 11.5 Points, Lines, and Rays

Read the problem carefully and solve. Show your work under each question.

Brian makes a drawing on graph paper. He uses a ruler to make his drawing.

Helpful Hint

A **point** is an exact location in space.

A **line** goes in both directions with no endpoints.

A **line segment** is part of a line. It has two endpoints.

A **ray** is a line that has one endpoint. It continues on and on in one direction.

A **vertex** is a point formed by two rays sharing a common endpoint.

1. Brian starts by drawing a point. Draw a point below.

2. Brian uses the point he drew to make a line segment. Draw a line segment below.

3. Brian draws the two rays below. Both rays share the same endpoint. What is this endpoint called?

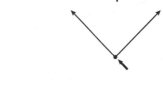

_____

4. Brian draws the figure below. What is the name of this figure?

_____

Lesson 11.6 Identifying Angles

Read the problem carefully and solve. Show your work under each question.

Cassandra makes a design for the cover of her journal. She uses a ruler to draw different types of angles to make her design.

Helpful Hint

An **angle** is formed from two rays with the same vertex.

A **right angle** makes a square corner. This type of angle is shown like this:

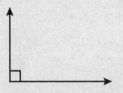

An **acute angle** is smaller than a right angle.

An **obtuse angle** is larger than a right angle.

1. Cassandra draws the angle below. What type of angle does she draw?

_____

2. Cassandra draws another angle shown below. What type of angle does she draw?

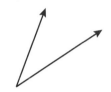

_____

3. Cassandra draws a right angle. Draw a right angle in the space below.

4. Cassandra draws an acute angle next. Draw an acute angle in the space below.

Lesson 11.9 Measuring Angles

Read the problem carefully and solve. Show your work under each question.

The Builtwell Home Design firm creates home plans for builders. Each home plan has many different angles. The students in a math class at Allendale School locate and name the angles on a set of blueprints.

Helpful Hint

A **protractor** is a tool used to measure angles.

Angles are measured in degrees.

A **right angle** measures exactly 90°.

An **acute angle** measures less than 90°.

An **obtuse angle** measures more than 90° but less than 180°.

1. Vanessa finds an angle at the edge of the roof that looks like the angle in the diagram below. What kind of angle is it?

 _____ angle

2. Kent sees an angle formed by the wall and floor. A picture of the angle is shown below. What is this angle called?

 _____ angle

3. Joseph identifies the angle at the peak of the roof. A picture of the angle is shown below. What kind of angle is this?

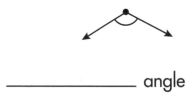

_____ angle

4. Rosina measures the angle in the diagram below. This angle represents how two of the walls meet in the home plan. Use a protractor to measure and name the angle.

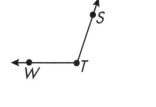

_____ _____ angle

5. Mato looks at an angle in a plan for a railing on a deck. What is the measure of the angle? Using the labels, what is the name of this angle?

_____ _____

Lesson 11.8 Adding Angles

Read the problem carefully and solve. Show your work under each question.

If the measurement of one angle is known, the measurement of the other angle can be found.

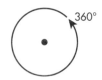

$x = 50°$
because
$90° - 40° = 50°$

A 360° rotation
about a point makes
a complete circle.

Find the unknown angles in the problems below.

---

1. A water sprinkler covers 90° of a lawn. How many more degrees would it need to cover in order to water half, or 180°, of the lawn?

_____

3. At her ice skating lesson, Jan attempts to do a 360° spin. She only does a 180° turn. How many degrees short of her goal was she?

_____

2. A ceiling fan rotates 30° and then stops. How many more degrees does it need to rotate in order to make it to 90°?

_____

4. Tom is editing a photograph. He rotates it 155° clockwise. He then rotates it another 50° clockwise. How many more degrees does Tom need to rotate the photograph to have made a 270° turn?

_____

Lesson 11.9 Parallel and Perpendicular Lines

Read the problem carefully and solve. Show your work under each question.

Victor draws a map of the streets near his school. He represents the streets using lines. He uses parallel lines, intersecting lines, and perpendicular lines to show how the streets look in the area.

Helpful Hint

Parallel lines never intersect, or cross over, each other. They are always the same distance apart.

Intersecting lines cross over each other.

Perpendicular lines intersect each other to form right angles.

1. Victor draws the pair of lines below. Identify these lines as parallel, intersecting, or perpendicular.

_____

2. Victor draws two lines that are parallel. Draw a set of parallel lines in the space below.

3. Victor draws the pair of lines below. Identify these lines as parallel, intersecting, or perpendicular.

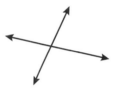

_____

4. Victor draws two lines that are perpendicular. Draw two lines that are perpendicular in the space below.

Lesson 11.10 Line Symmetry

Read the problem carefully and solve. Show your work under each question.

Line symmetry is when one side is a reflection (mirror-like) of the other side. The line of symmetry is the imaginary line where you could fold the image and have both halves match exactly. This rhombus has two equal sides.

Do the shapes below have a line, or lines, of symmetry? How many? Draw them.

1.

_____

4.

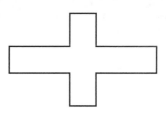

_____

2.

_____

5.

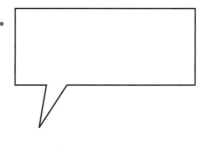

_____

3.

_____

6.

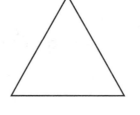

_____

Lesson 11.11 Ordered Pairs on a Coordinate Plane

Read the problem carefully and solve. Show your work under each question.

Sarah decides to show the location of some places in her neighborhood using a grid. She locates these places by plotting and labeling the points on the grid.

Helpful Hint

On a grid, the x axis runs on a horizontal line. The y axis runs on a vertical line.

A point on a grid is located by using an ordered pair. An ordered pair lists a point on the x axis first, then one on the y axis: (5, 3).

Points located on the same grid are called **coordinate points** or **coordinates**.

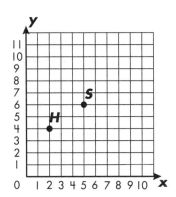

Use the grid above to answer each question.

1. Sarah plots her house on the grid. She labels the point H. What ordered pair represents point H?

   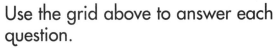

2. Sarah also plots her school on the grid. She labels the point S. What ordered pair represents point S?

   _____

3. Sarah wants to plot her friend Lisa's house at (3, 10) on the grid. She plans to label the point L. Plot the ordered pair (3, 10) on the grid above and label the point L.

4. Sarah loves to take her dog to the park. She plots the park on her grid at (9, 1), and labels the point P. Plot the ordered pair (9, 1) on the grid and label the point P.

Check What You Learned

Geometry

Read the problem carefully and solve. Show your work under each question.

Victor decides to make another street map. This time he wants to show his route to school. He plans to draw the streets near his house and around the school. Victor wants to use a grid to make his map. He plans to represent the streets using lines as he did before.

1. Victor plots a point on the grid below. What ordered pair represents this point?

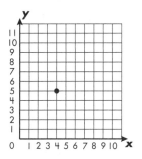

_____

2. Victor decides to draw a line segment using the point he just made. Use the point in the grid above to draw a line segment.

3. Victor wants to show an intersection of two streets. He draws two lines that are perpendicular to each other. Draw two lines that are perpendicular in the space below.

4. Victor draws the angle below. Identify the angle as a right angle, an obtuse angle, or an acute angle.

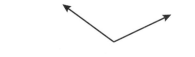

_____

Check What You Learned

Geometry

Read the problem carefully and solve. Show your work under each question.

Rose and Ann make a collage using different polygons. They cut out the shapes from colored paper. Then, they glue the shapes onto a large piece of paper in an interesting design.

1. Rose draws the polygon below on red paper. What is the name of this polygon?

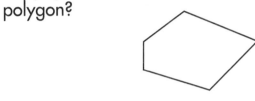

_____

3. Rose draws the two rectangles below on blue paper. She draws the rectangle on the left first. Did Rose slide, flip, or turn the first rectangle to make the second rectangle?

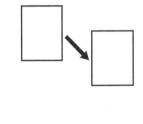

_____

2. Ann draws the two polygons below on yellow paper. Identify the shapes as congruent or not congruent.

_____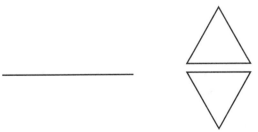

4. Ann gets a pair of scissors out of her pencil box to cut the shapes. Ann's pencil box reminds Rose of the solid figure below. What is the name of this figure?

_____

NAME _____

Check What You Know

Preparing for Algebra

Read the problem carefully and solve. Show your work under each question.

Nina and Calvin work on a math project together. They write examples of different types of patterns and number sentences.

---

1. Nina writes the number sentence below. Find the missing number in Nina's number sentence.

$(24 + 17) + 38 = (17 + 38) + \boxed{}$

2. Calvin writes the number sentence below. Find the missing number in Calvin's number sentence.

$4 \times 9 = 6 \times \boxed{}$

3. Calvin writes a number pattern. Complete Calvin's number pattern below.

12, 15, 19, $\boxed{}$, 30, $\boxed{}$, $\boxed{}$

4. Nina makes the pattern below using shapes. One of the shapes does not fit her pattern. Cross out this shape. Draw the correct shape on the blank line.

Describe what you notice about the pattern.

_____

_____

NAME _____

Lesson 12.1 Repeating Number Patterns

Read the problem carefully and solve. Show your work under each question.

The students in Mr. Lopez's class learn about repeating number patterns. Each student writes a repeating number pattern. The students leave some numbers missing from their pattern. Then, each student goes up to the board and shares his or her number pattern with the class.

Helpful Hint

To find the missing number in a set of numbers, look for repeating numbers and a repeating pattern.

1. Ben shares his number pattern with the class. Complete Ben's number pattern shown below.

7, 3, 7, 5, 7, 3, 7, ☐ , 7, 3, ☐ , 5

2. Lien shares her number pattern. Complete Lien's number pattern shown below.

150, 279, 150, 279, ☐ , ☐ , ☐

3. Tyrell shares his number pattern next. Complete Tyrell's number pattern shown below.

63, 42, 27, 12, 63,

42, ☐ , ☐ , ☐

4. Ariana shares her number pattern with the class. Complete Ariana's number pattern shown below.

20, 200, 30, 300,

☐ , 200, ☐ , ☐

Describe what you notice about the pattern.

_____

_____

Lesson 12.2 Growing Number Patterns

Read the problem carefully and solve. Show your work under each question.

Mr. Lopez's class also studies growing number patterns. Mr. Lopez divides the class into partners. Each student writes a growing number pattern. The students are told to leave some numbers missing from their pattern. Then, the students switch number patterns with their partners and fill in the missing numbers.

Helpful Hint

To find a missing number in a pattern:

1. Find the difference between numbers that are next to each other. Remember to check more than one pair of numbers.

2. Look at the differences between the numbers to find the pattern.

3. Add or subtract to find the missing numbers.

1. Tyrell gives his number pattern to his partner. Complete Tyrell's number pattern shown below.

13, 14, 16, 19, ☐ , ☐ , ☐

2. Maria writes the number pattern shown below and gives it to her partner. Complete Maria's number pattern.

240, 230, 210, ☐ , 140, ☐

3. Steve gives his number pattern to his partner. Complete Steve's number pattern shown below.

1036, 1021, 991, ☐ , ☐

4. Marcia writes the number pattern shown below and gives it to her partner. Complete Marcia's number pattern.

☐ , ☐ , 31, 40, 52, 67

Describe what you notice about the pattern.

_____

_____

Lesson 12.3 Geometric Patterns

Read the problem carefully and solve. Show your work under each question.

Emily and Sandy make bracelets to sell at the craft fair. They use beads with a variety of designs and shapes to make the bracelets. They string the beads in a different pattern for each bracelet.

Helpful Hint

Remember to look closely at each object in a geometric pattern. This will help you decide which object should come next in the pattern.

1. Emily lines up the beads she will use for her first bracelet. The pattern below shows the design she will use to string the beads. Draw the next two beads in this pattern.

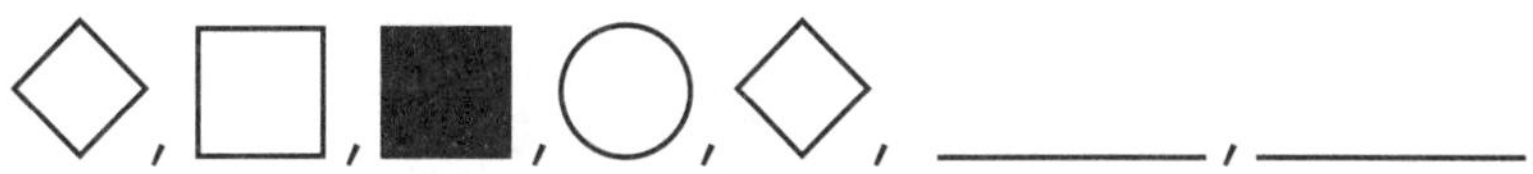

◇, □, ■, ○, ◇, _____ , _____

2. Sandy lines up the beads below for her first bracelet. She uses the pattern shown below to string the beads. Draw the next two beads in Sandy's pattern.

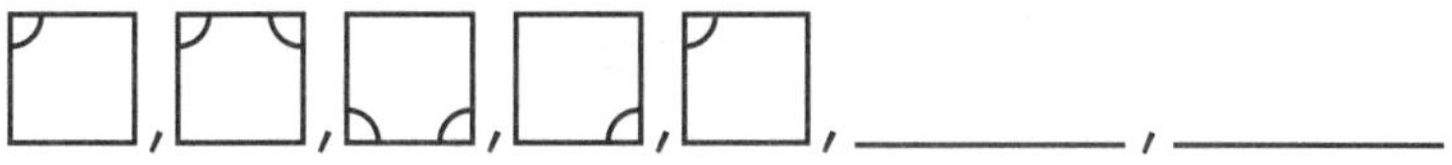

_____ , _____

3. Emily will use the pattern of beads shown below to make the next bracelet. Draw the next two beads in Emily's pattern.

○, ⊕, ◒, ◓, ●, _____ , _____

4. Sandy will use the pattern of beads shown below to make her next bracelet. Emily notices that one of the beads does not fit the pattern. Cross out this bead. Draw the correct bead on the blank line.

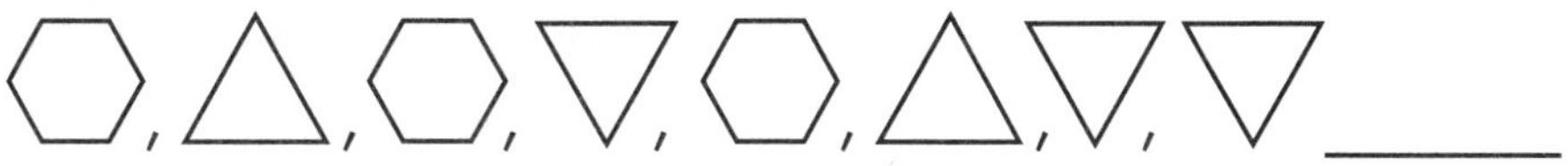

⬡, △, ⬡, ▽, ⬡, △, ▽, ▽ _____

Check What You Learned

Preparing for Algebra

Read the problem carefully and solve. Show your work under each question.

Enrica and Martin play another round of the missing number game. Then, they play the same game using patterns instead of number sentences. Enrica creates a pattern with a missing number or shape. Martin needs to find the missing number or shape. Then, he gets to create a pattern for Enrica to solve.

1. Enrica writes the number sentence below for Martin to solve. Find the missing number in Enrica's number sentence.

$$(34 \times 9) \times \boxed{} = (9 \times 12) \times 34$$

2. Martin writes the number sentence below for Enrica to solve. Find the missing number in Martin's number sentence.

$$5 \times 6 = 3 \times \boxed{}$$

3. Enrica writes a number pattern for Martin to solve. Complete Enrica's number pattern.

$$96, 92, 84, \boxed{}, \boxed{}$$

4. Martin creates the pattern below using shapes. One of the shapes does not fit the pattern. Cross out this shape. Draw the correct shape on the blank line.

_____

Describe why that shape does not fit the pattern.

_____

_____

Final Test Chapters 1–12

Read the problem carefully and solve. Show your work under each question.

Keri makes trail mix for a hiking trip. She plans to make enough batches of trail mix to share with some of her friends.

---

1. Keri uses $\frac{3}{4}$ cup of raisins in one batch of trail mix. How many cups of raisins does she use in 3 batches?

   _____ cups

2. Keri uses $\frac{3}{8}$ pound of peanuts for her first batch of trail mix. She uses $\frac{2}{8}$ pound of peanuts for the second batch. How much peanuts altogether did she use for both batches of trail mix?

   _____ pound

3. Keri uses two different kinds of dried fruit in the trail mix. She makes some of the batches with dried apples and some with dried pears. After making a few batches, Keri has $\frac{3}{8}$ pound of dried apples left. She has $\frac{2}{8}$ pound of dried pears left. Compare the two fractions using $<$, $>$, or $=$.

   _____

4. Keri puts the trail mix in small plastic bags for her 5 friends. She makes 18 bags of trail mix. She wants to give each friend an equal number of bags. How many bags will each friend get? How many will be left over?

   _____ bags _____ bags left

Spectrum Word Problems
Grade 4

Final Test
Chapters 1–12

107

CHAPTERS 1–12 FINAL TEST

Final Test Chapters 1–12

Read the problem carefully and solve. Show your work under each question.

Tyrone owns a fruit stand. He needs to order more fruit. He looks at his sales from last month to help him decide what kinds of fruit he should order for the fruit stand.

1. Tyrone sold $\frac{3}{10}$ of all his packages of strawberries in the first week of the month. How can $\frac{3}{10}$ be written as a decimal?

    _____

3. Tyrone looks at the total monthly sales of apples and pears. He finds that he made $1,089.13 in apple sales and $417.84 in pear sales. What is the difference between these two amounts?

    _____

2. Tyrone notices that he sold 9.43 pounds of blueberries last month. He also sold 9.34 pounds of raspberries. Compare the two decimals using <, >, or =.

    _____

4. Tyrone calculates that his total monthly fruit sales equal $21,780.49. Which digit is in the ten thousands place? Which digit is in the hundredths place?

    The digit in the ten thousands place

    is _____.

    The digit in the hundredths place

    is _____.

Final Test Chapters 1–12

Read the problem carefully and solve. Show your work under each question.

Joanne helps her dad make some birdhouses for their yard. Her dad plans to make the birdhouses out of wood. Joanne and her dad collect all the materials and supplies.

1. Joanne's dad gets a long piece of wood to cut into pieces to make the birdhouses. The piece of wood is 3 meters long. What is this length in centimeters?

_____ cm

3. Joanne and her dad buy a large bag of wild birdseed. The bag is labeled in ounces instead of pounds. It weighs 240 ounces. How much does the bag of wild birdseed weigh in pounds?

_____ lb.

2. Joanne's dad makes a roof for one of the birdhouses. The roof looks like the solid figure below. What is the name of this figure?

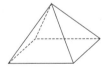

_____

4. Joanne and her dad also get a birdbath for their yard. The birdbath holds 2 gallons of water. How many quarts of water does it hold?

_____ qt.

Spectrum Word Problems
Grade 4

Final Test
Chapters 1–12

CHAPTERS 1–12 FINAL TEST

109

Final Test Chapters 1–12

Read the problem carefully and solve. Show your work under each question.

Claudia works at a furniture store. The store had a sale on couches, chairs, and tables for one week. Claudia made the graph to the right to show the number of couches, tables, and chairs the store sold during that sale week.

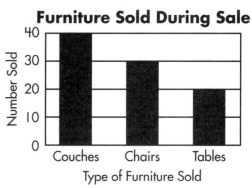

Furniture Sold During Sale

1. What type of furniture did the store sell the most of during the sale week?

   _____

3. How many more couches did the store sell than tables during the sale week?

   _____ couches

2. How many chairs did the store sell during the sale week?

   _____ chairs

4. After the sale, the store receives a delivery of 20 round tables in separate boxes. Thirteen tables have light-colored wood, and 7 tables have dark-colored wood. If Claudia chooses a box without looking, what is the probability she will choose a table with dark-colored wood?

   _____

Spectrum Word Problems
Grade 4
110

CHAPTERS 1-12 FINAL TEST

Final Test
Chapters 1–12

Final Test Chapters 1–12

Read the problem carefully and solve. Show your work under each question.

Miguel is remodeling a park. He plans to have two gardens and a fountain. He draws and labels a model of the area for the large garden on a coordinate grid. He also draws a model for the small garden and for the fountain.

---

1. Miguel draws a model of the large garden on the grid below. He plots and labels the five points. Then, he connects them with straight lines. What ordered pair represents point A?

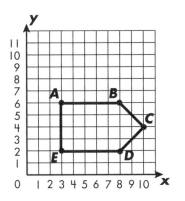

_____

2. Look at the model of the garden above. What is the name of this polygon?

_____

3. Miguel starts to draw a model of a small garden. He draws the angle below. Identify his angle as a right angle, an obtuse angle, or an acute angle.

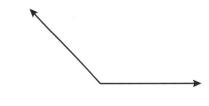

_____

4. Miguel wants to put a fountain in the center of the park. The fountain will be in a rectangular shaped pool. The length of the pool will be 25 feet. The width of the pool will be 14 feet. What is the perimeter of the pool? What is the area of the pool?

The perimeter of the pool is

_____ feet.

The area of the pool is _____ square feet.

Spectrum Word Problems
Grade 4

Final Test
Chapters 1–12

111

CHAPTERS 1–12 FINAL TEST

NAME _____

Final Test Chapters 1–12

Read the problem carefully and solve. Show your work under each question.

Andrea and her friend Patrick learn about patterns and number sentences in their math class. They each decide to make a book of math puzzles for the other to solve.

1. Andrea writes a number pattern. Complete Andrea's number pattern below.

   64, 55, 47, 40, ☐ , ☐ , ☐

   Describe what you notice about the pattern.

   _____

   _____

2. Patrick writes the number sentence below. Find the missing number in Patrick's number sentence.

   $(34 + 27) + 19 = (27 + 19) + $ ☐

3. Andrea writes the pattern below using shapes. One of the shapes does not fit her pattern. Cross out this shape. Draw the correct shape on the blank line.

   _____

4. Patrick writes the number sentence below. Find the missing number in Patrick's number sentence.

   $12 \times 7 = 96 - $ ☐

Spectrum Word Problems
Grade 4
112

Final Test
Chapters 1–12

CHAPTERS 1–12 FINAL TEST

Scoring Record for Posttests, Mid-Test, and Final Test

Chapter Posttest	Your Score	Performance			
		Excellent	Very Good	Fair	Needs Improvement
1	____ of 4	4	3	2	1
2	____ of 4	4	3	2	1
3	____ of 4	4	3	2	1
4	____ of 4	4	3	2	1
5	____ of 4	4	3	2	1
6	____ of 4	4	3	2	1
7	____ of 8	7–8	5–6	3–4	2 or fewer
8	____ of 4	4	3	2	1
9	____ of 4	4	3	2	1
10	____ of 8	7–8	5–6	3–4	2 or fewer
11	____ of 8	7–8	5–6	3–4	2 or fewer
12	____ of 4	4	3	2	1
Mid-Test	____ of 16	15–16	13–14	11–12	10 or fewer
Final Test	____ of 24	22–24	20–21	16–19	15 or fewer

Record your test score in the Your Score column. See where your score falls in the Performance columns. Your score is based on the total number of required responses. If your score is fair or needs improvement, review the chapter material.

Grade 4 Answers

Chapter 1

Pretest, page 1
1. 227
2. 57
3. 254
4. 38; 38 + 84 = 122

Lesson 1.1, page 2
1. 7
2. 18
3. 21
4. 39

Lesson 1.2, page 3
1. 3
2. 10
3. 2
4. 12

Lesson 1.3, page 4
1. 18; 7 + 3 and 4 + 4
2. lower; 16
3. 17
4. 19

Lesson 1.4, page 5
1. 44
2. 36
3. 80
4. after

Lesson 1.5, page 6
1. 57
2. sixth
3. 66
4. 260

Lesson 1.6, page 7
1. 175
2. 128
3. 69
4. 35

Lesson 1.7, page 8
1. 101 − 23 = 78
2. 95; 95 + 18 = 113
3. 17; 17 + 84 = 101

Posttest, page 9
1. 211
2. 45
3. 260
4. 59; 59 + 94 = 153

Chapter 2

Pretest, page 10
1. 700,000
2. 1,000,000 I 60,000 I 8,000 I 300 I 50 I 2; one million sixty-eight thousand three hundred fifty-two.
3. 983,832 < 984,421
4. 1,070,000

Lesson 2.1, page 11
1. 900
2. 4; 40,000
3. 60,000 + 8,000 + 900 + 50 + 4; sixty-eight thousand nine hundred fifty-four
4. 9; 9,000

Lesson 2.2, page 12
1. 700,000
2. Devin; 9,000
3. 800,000 + 70,000 + 3,000 + 400+ 60 + 5
4. 400,000 +90,000 + 1,000 + 600 + 20 + 7

Lesson 2.3, page 13
1. 2,000,000
2. this; 70,000
3. 2,000,000 + 600,000 + 70,000 + 500 + 3
4. 2,000,000 + 700,000 + 8,000 + 30 + 4

Lesson 2.4, page 14
1. 837,000
2. 120,000
3. 2,000,000
4. 124,000

Lesson 2.5, page 15
1. <
2. 1,942 > 1,493
3. 542,002 < 572,184
4. Lee; 3,892,356 > 3,891,936

Posttest, page 16
1. 30,000
2. 2,000,000 + 500,000 + 80,000 + 400 + 90; two million five hundred eighty thousand four hundred ninety
3. 32,961 > 32,053
4. 2,700,000

Chapter 3

Pretest, page 17
1. 13,532
2. 2,138
3. 9,000
4. 24,926

Grade 4 Answers

Lesson 3.1, page 18
1. 917
2. 703
3. 1,620
4. 454

Lesson 3.2, page 19
1. 322
2. 1,151
3. 1,576
4. 2,395

Lesson 3.3, page 20
1. 11,301
2. 72,356
3. 83,657
4. 34,926

Lesson 3.4, page 21
1. 1,919
2. 1,018
3. Kim's
4. Roberto's

Lesson 3.5, page 22
1. 1,126
2. 2,486
3. 2,261

Lesson 3.6, page 23
1. 4,000
2. 2,000
3. 18,000
4. 6,000

Posttest, page 24
1. 15,620
2. 3,418
3. 11,000
4. 27,822

Chapter 4

Pretest, page 25
1. 945
2. 6,105
3. 120
4. 665

Lesson 4.1, page 26
1. 72
2. 36
3. 36
4. 56; 64

Lesson 4.2, page 27
1. 96
2. 69
3. 64; 46
4. 99

Lesson 4.3, page 28
1. 742; 423
2. 1,672
3. 318
4. 329

Lesson 4.4, page 29
1. 273
2. 231
3. 299
4. 384

Lesson 4.5, page 30
1. 2,312
2. 1,222
3. 2,108
4. 1,300

Lesson 4.6, page 31
1. 9,417
2. 3,456
3. 2,432
4. 4,816

Posttest, page 32
1. 1,615
2. 4,060
3. Jackson Building; 1,615
4. 3,335

Chapter 5

Pretest, page 33
1. 9
2. 9
3. 8; $3 \times 8 = 24$
4. 6

Lesson 5.1, page 34
1. 2
2. 4
3. 5
4. 4

Grade 4 Answers

Lesson 5.2, page 35
1. 9
2. 8
3. 7
4. 7

Lesson 5.3, page 36
1. 9
2. 8
3. $7 \times 8 = 56$
4. 5

Posttest, page 37
1. 8
2. 8
3. $9; 7 \times 9 = 63$
4. 5

Chapter 6

Pretest, page 38
1. 14; 5
2. 4; 5; The bookstore will need 1 extra box to ship the remaining 3 books.
3. 23; 6
4. Yes, all the books will fit. There will be 36 books in each box with no books left over.

Lesson 6.1, page 39
1. 3; 1
2. 4; Her team will need 1 extra car to bring the remaining player.
3. No, her team does not have enough cars. Two players will still need a ride.
4. 11; 1

Lesson 6.2, page 40
1. 34; 2
2. 27; 0
3. No, Natalia does not have enough pages because there will be 3 stamps left over. She will need 1 extra page for a total of 6 pages.

Posttest, page 41
1. 6; 5
2. 24; 25
3. 18; 0
4. 101; 1

Mid-Test

Page 42
1. 10,405
2. 34,945
3. 30,000
4. 39,601

Page 43
1. 30,000
2. $9,403,876 < 9,430,523$
3. $9,000,000 + 400,000 + 3,000 + 800 + 70 + 6$
4. 9,400,000

Page 44
1. 754
2. 5,510
3. 144
4. 572

Page 45
1. 95; 3
2. 119; 0
3. 27; 2
4. 239

Chapter 7

Pretest, page 46
1.
2. $\frac{5}{8} < \frac{7}{8}$
3. $\frac{6}{9}$
4. $\frac{6}{7}$

Pretest, page 47
1. 0.9
2. $4.29 < 4.92$
3. 0.57
4. $42.94

Lesson 7.1, page 48
1.   2.
3.   4.

Grade 4 Answers

Lesson 7.2, page 49
1.
2.
3.
4.

Lesson 7.3, page 50
1. $\frac{3}{5} > \frac{2}{5}$
2. $\frac{4}{8} < \frac{6}{8}$
3. $\frac{3}{4} = \frac{3}{4}$
4. $\frac{2}{7} < \frac{5}{7}$

Lesson 7.4, page 51
1. $5\frac{4}{5}$
2. $9\frac{1}{2}$
3. $7\frac{1}{5}$
4. $9\frac{2}{5}$
5. $5\frac{1}{3}$

Lesson 7.5, page 52
1.
2. $\frac{4}{5}$
3.
4. $\frac{2}{6}$ or $\frac{1}{3}$

Lesson 7.6, page 53
1. $\frac{12}{20}$
2. $\frac{15}{21}$
3. $\frac{2}{3}$
4. $\frac{4}{5}$

Lesson 7.7, page 54
1. $\frac{6}{8}$
2. $\frac{3}{4}$
3. $\frac{7}{9}$
4. $\frac{7}{10}$

Lesson 7.8, page 55
1. $\frac{5}{9}$
2. $\frac{4}{12}$
3. $\frac{2}{8}$
4. $\frac{4}{6}$

Lesson 7.9, page 56
1. $1\frac{4}{5}$
2. $2\frac{1}{7}$
3. $1\frac{7}{9}$
4. $1\frac{2}{5}$
5. 2

Lesson 7.10, page 57
1. $\frac{90}{100}$ or $\frac{9}{10}$
2. $\frac{70}{100}$ or $\frac{7}{10}$; 0.7
3. 0.5
4. $\frac{3}{10}$

Lesson 7.11, page 58
1. 15
2. $18 = 2 \times 3 \times 3$
3. 8, 9, 15, 18, 22
4. 11

Lesson 7.12, page 59
1. $549.42
2. $2,241.81
3. $136.07
4. $958.96

Posttest, page 60
1.
2. $\frac{4}{6} > \frac{3}{6}$
3. $\frac{15}{20}$
4. $\frac{2}{6}$

Posttest, page 61
1. 0.8
2. 21.86 > 21.68 cm
3. 23.28
4. $17.55

Grade 4 Answers

Chapter 8

Pretest, page 62
1. 24; 20
2. 4
3. 80
4. 10

Lesson 8.1, page 63
1. $2\frac{1}{2}$
2. ───────────
3. $1\frac{1}{8}$
4. ───────────

Lesson 8.2, page 64
1. 3
2. 21
3. 48
4. 15,840

Lesson 8.3, page 65
1. 36; 48; 60; 72
2. 56
3. 5 ft. 1 in.
4. 54

Lesson 8.4, page 66
1. $1\times$ over $2\frac{1}{4}$, $1\times$ over $2\frac{2}{4}$, $3\times$s over $3\frac{1}{4}$, $1\times$ over 4
2. $1\frac{3}{4}$
3. $3\frac{1}{4}$
4. 5

Lesson 8.5, page 67
1. 3
2. 32
3. 3
4. 48

Lesson 8.6, page 68
1. 12,000
2. 3
3. 32
4. 4,800

Lesson 8.7, page 69
1. 20
2. 28
3. 44
4. 16

Lesson 8.8, page 70
1. 42
2. 112
3. 36
4. 8

Posttest, page 71
1. 216; 66
2. 6,000
3. 12
4. 45

Chapter 9

Pretest, page 72
1. 26; 36
2. 300
3. 7,000
4. 3,000

Lesson 9.1, page 73
1. ───────────
2. 120
3. 50
4. 9

Lesson 9.2, page 74
1. 3
2. 400
3. 2
4. 8,000

Lesson 9.3, page 75
1. 150
2. 3
3. 2,000
4. 4,000

Lesson 9.4, page 76
1. 2,000
2. 4,000
3. 14,000
4. 18

Lesson 9.5, page 77
1. 2
2. 300,000
3. 5,000
4. 135,000

Lesson 9.6, page 78
1. 75
2. 132
3. 95
4. 200

Grade 4 Answers

Posttest, page 79
1. 400
2. 38; 84
3. 200,000
4. 5,000

Chapter 10

Pretest, page 80
1. Tuesday
2. 10
3. 15
4. $\frac{7}{12}$

Pretest, page 81
1. 4
2. 20
3. 1; 3
4. $\frac{9}{25}$

Lesson 10.1, page 82
1. summer
2. 15
3. winter
4. 6

Lesson 10.2, page 83
1. 4
2. 2
3. 2; 3
4. 4

Lesson 10.3, page 84
1. $\frac{1}{8}$
2. $\frac{5}{8}$
3. $\frac{4}{8}$
4. $\frac{2}{8}$

Posttest, page 85
1. fiction; nonfiction
2. 5
3. 4
4. $\frac{13}{20}$

Posttest, page 86
1. 3
2. 60
3. 40
4. $\frac{11}{140}$

Chapter 11

Pretest, page 87
1. (3, 3)
2. Answers may vary.

3. ⟷
   ⟷
4. right angle

Pretest, page 88
1. hexagon
2. not congruent
3. flip
4. cylinder

Lesson 11.1, page 89
1. octagon
2. ⬠ ; pentagon
3. ⬠ ; hexagon
4. quadrilateral

Lesson 11.2, page 90
1. cone
2. sphere
3. rectangular prism
4. square pyramid

Lesson 11.3, page 91
1. congruent
2. not congruent
3. not congruent
4. congruent

Grade 4 Answers

Lesson 11.4, page 92

1. turn
2.

3.

4.

Lesson 11.5, page 93

1. ●
2. ●————————●
3. vertex
4. line

Lesson 11.6, page 94

1. obtuse angle
2. acute angle
3.

4. Answers may vary.

Lesson 11.7, page 95

1. acute
2. right
3. obtuse
4. 110°; obtuse
5. 90°; ∠678

Lesson 11.8, page 96

1. 90°
2. 60°
3. 180°
4. 65°

Lesson 11.9, page 97

1. perpendicular
2.
3. intersecting
4.

Lesson 11.10, page 98

1. yes; 1
2. no
3. yes; 4
4. yes; 2
5. no
6. yes; 3

Lesson 11.11, page 99

1. (2,4)
2. (5,6)
3.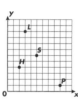
4.

Posttest, page 100

1. (4, 5)
2. Answers may vary.

3.
4. obtuse angle

Posttest, page 101

1. pentagon
2. congruent
3. slide
4. rectangular prism

Spectrum Word Problems
Grade 4
120

Answer Key

Grade 4 Answers

Chapter 12

Pretest, page 102
1. 24
2. 6
3. 24; 37; 45
4. cross out fifth shape; ⬠; The pattern is triangle, hexagon, circle, and then it repeats over and over.

Lesson 12.1, page 103
1. 5; 7
2. 150; 279; 150
3. 27; 12; 63
4. 20; 30; 300; The pattern repeats. It is 20, 200, 30, 300, and then repeats.

Lesson 12.2, page 104
1. 23; 28; 34
2. 180; 90
3. 946; 886
4. 22; 25; I had to subtract 6 to find the second number, and subtract 3 to find the first number.

Lesson 12.3, page 105
1. ▢▨

2. ◹, ◺

3. ◯, ◔

4. cross out seventh shape; ⬡

Posttest, page 106
1. 12
2. 10
3. 72; 56
4. cross out sixth circle; ⊕; Because the pattern is 1 dot, 2 dots, 3 dots, 4 dots, and the shape I crosssed out should have 2 dots to be corrrect.

Final Test

Page 107
1. $2\frac{1}{4}$
2. $\frac{5}{8}$
3. $\frac{2}{8} < \frac{3}{8}$
4. 3; 3

Page 108
1. 0.3
2. 9.43 > 9.34
3. $671.29
4. 2; 9

Page 109
1. 300
2. square pyramid
3. 15
4. 8

Page 110
1. couches
2. 30
3. 20
4. $\frac{7}{20}$

Page 111
1. (3,6)
2. pentagon
3. obtuse
4. 78; 350

Page 112
1. 34; 29; 25; The pattern is to subtract 9 from the first number to get the second number, then 8 to get the next, then 7, 6, 5, and 4.
2. 34
3. cross out the third shape; ▦

   or cross out the last shape; ▦
4. 12

Notes

Notes

Notes